ARDUINO
PROGRAMMING
FOR BEGINNERS

A Comprehensive Beginner's Guide to Learn the
Realms of Arduino Programming from A-Z

ADA PROTOSMITH

Table of Contents

Introduction

Today's world is built off basic technology. Switches, resisters, circuits, and boards allow electrical current to travel to specific places within a device resulting in specific actions taking place. An example of this would be a light switch. When we flip a light switch in either direction, we will either turn on the light or turn it off. Understanding why this occurs and what can be done with this simple technology is the basis for tools like the Arduino.

What Is an Arduino?

An Arduino is a low-cost open-source microcontroller board which is programmed using the Arduino IDE. It is basically a microprocessor with I/O pins that allows you to control external devices and sensors. You can use it to create anything from a simple robot to a complex video game. The Arduino is designed to be used with other electronic components such as resistors, capacitors, transistors, LEDs, push buttons, and relays. The Arduino can also be used with temperature sensors, accelerometers, GPS modules, etc.

Why Do We Need an Arduino?

In its simplest form, an Arduino is a teaching tool. This device is small enough to fit into a shirt pocket and be taken into classrooms and other venues. The Arduino will teach children and adults how the basics of our world function and operates.

On top of this, the Arduino is fun. It is a great way to create things that are deep within our imaginations. Kids can purchase one of these devices and, after a few hours, create video games, robots, remote-controlled cars or anything that their imagination can dream up. The Arduino is popular over other development options because the end user doesn't have to write any programming code. This makes the barrier to entry much lower and more attractive to those who simply want to create something and have it work.

Who Should Use These?

Anyone who is interested in creating fun and engaging projects. This can be kids, adults, teachers, or professionals. These little devices can quickly become addicting and, when networked together, allow end users to create amazing projects.

Chapter 1

How Do I Get
Started with Arduino?

N ow that you have a basic understanding of what an Arduino is, the next step in the process is to determine the type of projects you are interested in creating. As a beginner, we highly recommend that you start with the most basic board or even a simple kit that will complete a specific project. In the beginning, your goal should be to get a feel and understanding of what is possible before jumping into more complex projects.

When starting out, people will look at all the cool things they can create with the board and want to jump in without knowing the basics. They will want to create killer robots or even the next Nintendo operating system. These are often ambitious goals for a newbie and, if attempted at this stage, could cause frustration and you will quickly lose interest.

For this reason, we will take a step back and go with the most basic of boards and tools needed. As you play and experiment, advance at your own pace, experimenting and pushing the limits of Arduino as you see fit.

The Boards

It all starts with the boards. The Arduino boards come in many sizes and flavors. Each will have more advanced technology, options, and capabilities built into them. When you begin to understand what each board is capable of, picking the right boards for your specific projects will become much easier.

Arduino Uno

The Arduino Uno is the most basic unit that is produced. It can run some basic sensors and simple applications and has an input voltage of 6-20V. Any higher voltage applied to this board can cause it to overheat, burn out, or suffer severe damage. It is vital that when using this board, you don't overload it.

The Uno has fourteen digital input/outputs, which will allow the user to get started with some basic projects. When working with these fourteen connections, ensure that you follow any directions correctly.

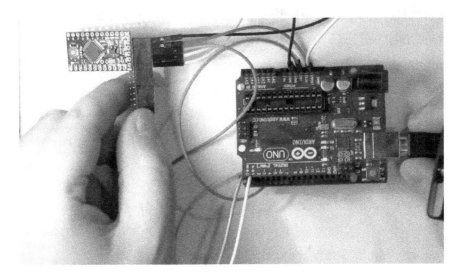

Arduino Micro

If you are looking to have a little more power and take up less space in your project, then the Arduino Micro may be a good option. With the Micro, you have twenty pins compared to the fourteen on the Uno. Also, the micro is smaller, which will allow the device to fit into smaller spaces if needed. Otherwise, the two boards are virtually the same.

Arduino Pro/Pro Micro

Stepping up in boards, we now have the Arduino Pro and Pro Micro. Adding to the features of the previous boards, the Pro is a full-sized board with some additional shields installed. The Pro Micro is like the Pro but with a smaller form factor.

Each board also comes with dual voltage options - 5 volt and 3.3 volt. These, again, will allow for additional projects to be created. One disadvantage of these boards is that they are not good at prototyping. Since they removed the headers from the boards, we can consider it a more advanced model to work with. The advantage is that with the headers removed, it is a good board to work with if you are looking to improve your soldering skills.

The clock speed on the boards is also different. If you purchase the 3.3 volt, you will have a clock speed of 8MHZ, whereas the 5 volt has a 16MHZ clock. This may not make too much of a difference but may hinder some projects.

Arduino Nano

The final board for beginners will be the Arduino Nano. This is a great board if you want the best of both worlds. The nano has the power and capabilities of the Uno and the size of the Micro.

More Advanced Boards

Once you have gotten your feet wet with the boards above, you can explore more of what boards are available in the Arduino family. New boards are being developed and made available to those into using these boards to build.

Some boards that you can look at will be the Mega, Leonardo, Due, Ethernet, & Yun. Each of these boards will increase your ability to create new and advanced projects. The main thing when looking for the right board is to pick one or two and try them out. Once you get a feeling for what is possible, then mixing and matching, playing with new configurations, and improving your skills will become second nature. Take it slow and have fun.

Software to Run Your Arduino

With any type of hardware, be it a computer, cell phone, or even the Arduino, we need software to achieve any type of functionality. We know the software that runs these devices as an operating system. The Arduino has its own operating system known as the Arduino IDE.

Local vs. Cloud-Based IDE

The Arduino comes with two versions of its IDE. The local version of the IDE will be downloaded and installed onto your physical computer, allowing you to work offline and without an Internet connection. This version is great if your Internet connection is slow or not as stable.

The cloud-based IDE is preferred. There are many advantages to using the cloud-based IDE over a local copy. When working in the cloud, the end user will always have the most stable and up-to-date version of the IDE. With the local copy, the user may constantly need to update their software.

The next advantage is that the code or "sketches" is stored on the cloud, making it accessible to anyone who has access to your account. This makes sharing code with others and retrieving code that's already been written much easier.

The user is given a web editor when working with the cloud-based version of the software. This web editor has a user-friendly interface making development fun and easy.

Getting the Software for Your Specific Board

With each board being slightly different, the need for a specific IDE is required. Installing or using the wrong IDE may cause the board to not function properly or even install on the device. The best thing that the user can do is visit the following website to retrieve the most up-to-date information on their specific board.

https://www.arduino.cc/en/Guide

Downloading the Version for Your Operating System

For those users that want to go with the local version of the IDE, it is important to choose the proper software for your computer's operating system. Since Arduino is an open-source project, it can run on multiple devices. These include Microsoft Windows, macOS, Linux, and portable versions of Windows and Linux.

For those working with the Chromebook, it is also possible to run the Arduino on that as well. Getting the specific IDE from the Chrome Web Store - Arduino Create will be necessary.

Getting Started with the Web-Based Editor

From this point forward, we will work with the web-based editor. Since the IDE is the same, the steps that follow will relate to any version of the IDE you use, local or cloud.

Creating an Account

The first thing you need to do is create an account with Arduino. This account will allow you to access all the tools and resources available to start and work on your projects. To do this, visit the following website.

https://www.arduino.cc/

In the far upper right-hand corner of the page, you will see "Sign In." Click on that link and you will be taken to the login form. If you previously created an account, enter your credentials in the white boxes. If this is your first time creating an account, locate "Create Account" under the Sign In button.

Other options for creating an account are to use either your Google, GitHub, Facebook, or Apple account logins. Either way, the results will create an account.

Login to the Editor

Once your account is created, you will need to confirm that you are creating the account. Also, you will receive access to the Forum, where you can read discussion posts, ask questions, and become part of the community. These credentials will also allow you to purchase products to increase your functionality and do different projects.

Once inside the editor, you will need to select the Operating System that you are currently using. If you are on Windows, choose that; if on something else, choose accordingly.

The last step is for the web editor to recognize your board. Connect your board according to the specific instructions given to you in the documentation. Once connected, the web IDE will detect the board, allowing you to start communicating and developing the projects you have in your head.

Setting up a Work Area

When working with electronics, you must work in a specific area of your home. Once you start getting into developing with Arduino, you will quickly become overwhelmed with the mess and clutter you will find yourself in. Now, this doesn't mean that you are a messy person; it simply means that you need to have a dedicated area to work, making life and development simple.

The Room

You will want to pick a dedicated room when working with your Arduino. Many developers will set up a space in the garage or a spare room. It is suggested that you work in a room that has no carpeting on the floor. The reason for this is that carpet can cause static electricity, which could cause damage to your electronics. Try to find a room with hardwood floors, linoleum, tile, or concrete surfaces. This will ensure that you have no issues.

The next thing that you want to take into consideration is power. You want to have a location where you can easily have access to power outlets. Adding in power strips and other surge protection is also a good idea. When designing your room, make sure that you have plenty of space for outlets and make it neat; you don't want wires running everywhere.

Lighting

The next component will be the lighting. You will be working with a lot of small objects such as transistors, LEDs, and more. Over time your eyes will become tired, and it will be difficult to see what is going on. For this reason, you want to have enough light to see your projects and the components you are working with.

Worktable

Make sure you are giving yourself enough room to work and stretch out. As you start developing your projects, you will quickly find that you need a lot of room to work. This can be for connecting components together or for your tools.

The worktable should be made from wood. Wood tables don't conduct electricity and are grounded. If you are working with a metal table, purchase a static rubber mat. This will be where you can work on your projects. A plastic table will also work; however, many of these are folding tables, and you don't want to have an issue with the table falling if the legs come loose.

Peg Board

A peg board will great hold your tools. You will be working with plyers, screw drivers, and even soldering irons as well. When you can hang and keep these items out of the way, it makes working on projects much easier.

Glass Jars and other storage containers

As you work with your Arduino, you will want to have a way to contain and maintain all the pieces and parts that you collect over time. Many of these items will have pins and other connectors that could become damaged if left out in the open. Find ways to keep everything together, clean and organized.

Comfortable Chair

As you slave away for hours at your craft, you want to ensure that you have a comfortable chair. This chair should be supportive and easy to move. If you start working on projects and your back starts to hurt, you will become stressed and possibly make mistakes. Be comfortable.

Rubber Foot Mat

You will want to find a rubber mat that you can roll around on and keep your feet comfortable. This mat should be blue or a dark color. The reason for this is that when you drop items, and you will, it will have a softer surface to fall on, and since it is blue or a darker color, it will be easier to spot components.

Whiteboard and Markers

As you work with the Arduino, you will want a place to work out your ideas and sketches. Typically, people will work with pen and paper, which is fine; however, having a large whiteboard will make designing your ideas much easier, and you can make changes without making a mess.

Whiteboards are also great for other tasks you may have working on. If you are working in a garage or other area, consider getting whiteboard paint; this way you can do the entire room. It not only looks cool, but people will think you are a mad scientist.

The markers you choose will also play a good role in your development. You can use different color markers to signify the different color wires that you use in your project. If you are running a red or blue wire, you can easily show it in your sketch.

Laptop stand or swing arm

As you develop with your Arduino, you will need to hook your device up to a computer. Many people will use laptops to code on. To help keep these devices out of the way, we can have a raised table secured to the wall, or we can install a swing arm that we can rest the laptop on. This will make development much easier and will keep the laptop in a safe and secure location as we work. If we have to keep moving the laptop as we code, it could easily become damaged or just an annoyance.

3D Printer

Developing and designing custom boxes and components will be a much-desired skill as you develop and become more proficient. When working with different projects, you may want to 3D print a car chassis or perhaps some random element to make a project look cool.

With the power of 3D printers, anything that we want to develop is now a reality. We are able to pull designs off the Internet and have them made in a few hours to a day or two. This will spark your creativity and give you unlimited possibilities for developing with your Arduino.

If you get a 3D printer, get a good one. Don't get the lowest model or something that will break easily. Since this is going to be a major component that you will use with or without your Arduino, do your research and find one that will be easy to use and last a long time.

Safety First

Finally, when developing your work area, you want to prioritize safety. You are working with electronics, and you don't want to damage them or want them to harm anyone else. Give yourself enough room to work and follow all shop rules. Creating with your Arduino should be fun and safe.

Purchasing Your Arduino

Now that you have a basic understanding of what an Arduino is, what it can do, and how you can connect it up and get it running, your next question might be, where can you get one?

There are many places online where you can get any type of board or accessory. You can visit https://www.arduino.cc/, which is the official location for these boards. Here you can find boards, kits, shields, and even retired equipment that is no longer supported but could be of use for past projects.

From there, searching sites like Amazon.com will bring you to their official store, where boards and other devices can be found at a discounted price. Since this is a huge hobby that has lots of people engaged, finding just the right board and kit shouldn't be difficult.

Key components that you will want to keep under consideration are libraries and drivers. Since the Arduino community is so large, there are written libraries to ensure that everything works and operates as it should. When looking for libraries, you want to consider how well documented they are. Since you are a new developer, you want to find well-documented libraries. This documentation will help ensure that your projects work right the first time and every time. There is nothing worse than working on a project only to discover that the code to run it is poorly written.

Have Fun

Finally, have fun. This should be fun, educational, and inspirational. When starting off with these kits, allow your imagination to run wild, and don't be afraid to take your ideas to the next level. As you develop and learn, you will discover tasks and projects you never thought of. Just because you don't see a specific need for a project at the moment, do it anyways. It will help you develop new skills and have a fresh outlook on developing projects.

Some of the greatest inspiration comes from experimentation. When you can get one thing to work in an area that you didn't think of, your skills can transfer over to a totally different project that wouldn't have been possible if you didn't experiment in the first place.

Chapter 2

The Basics

The Arduino web editor is where all the magic happens when working with your Arduino. In the editor, you connect to your device, use a simple builder to connect pieces and components together, set up simple sketches or commands that will trigger events when used, and even dive into more advanced programming options later in your exploration of the Arduino.

When starting out, take some time to poke around the interface. Take notes of what you see and where common tasks are located. Another thing you will want to do is take note of shortcuts. Shortcuts are keyboard commands that you can use to do common tasks. These might seem like insignificant items, but as you develop, they will quickly become useful and help with development and debugging time.

The Basics of Programming
Without making it too difficult, you can make things happen with your Arduino through programming. Programming is a series of commands written in a specific order that run or become active after the user does specific action.

You should look at it in this context. Pushing a button on your phone will cause an event in your phone's operating system to correspond to your desired action. It can turn down the volume, turn the phone off, or even answer a call. To make this happen, a developer or programmer needs to write code that speaks to the phone and then set a trigger to complete the task. The same thing will happen when you are working with your Arduino. We will create a series of commands in a specific order to accomplish the task. Trust me; it is simpler than it sounds.

Developing Sketches

We know the programming code to develop with your Arduino as sketches. These sketches are written using the web editor and saved with a special extension of .ino, the type of file your Arduino understands.

As a beginning developer, you should be looking for prewritten code or sketches that you can examine and learn from. When developing, learning how to read code and discover why things are done can help your comprehension when looking at future projects.

One thing that you will quickly want to learn is that most of the code to do a specific task has already been written in one form or another by someone else. Exploring what others have done and reading their comments in the code will help you understand and grow with the development process.

Preparing for Your First Program

It's at this point we are now ready to dive in and start developing our projects with the Arduino. The computer you are using should have the IDE installed and be in the editor. The next step is to connect your device physically to your computer.

Prewritten Examples

As you dive in and explore, understand that the IDE comes with a large collection of prewritten examples that you can look at and play with. You might want to take some time and simply open up a few of them before getting started. Take your time to learn the basics before diving in; it will save you hours of headache later.

Connecting Your Device

Supplied with your Arduino will be a standard USB cable. This cable will connect your Arduino to your computer. Take one end of the USB cable and connect it to the back of your computer into a USB port. Once secure, take the other end and plug it into your device.

When connecting with the Arduino, your computer will make the typical USB detection beep, letting you know it has found the device. If your computer does not do this, it may not have found the device. Ensure that your cables are secure, and try again if you are having problems.

Once your device is connected, we want to ensure that the IDE is picking up the device and it is picking up the correct one. If you are not, it will have to be selected at this point.

Loading Bare Minimum

When developing software or sketches, there are three ways that you can go about doing it. First, open a blank document and start writing your code from scratch. We do not recommend this method for those just starting out. In fact, the blank screen can seem fairly intimidating to most people.

The second way is to use code that another developer has created previously. This is where many people will turn to. This is a great way to learn and understand how sketches are written, why they work, and what to look for if you are experimenting with code. If a programmer sees that their code matches exactly what someone else has done, they can usually backtrack to determine what went wrong.

Finally, we can start with the bare minimum file. This file isn't a full-blown application but a sketch that all your applications and programs will use. In the world of programming, remember, never try to reinvent the wheel. If it has been written and it works, use it.

To pull up the bare minimum file, follow these steps.

```
File -> Examples -> Basic -> Bare Minimum
```

Once on that link, click it with your mouse to open. Once open, you will have the skeleton or framework for all sketches to work. Once open, you will see a file that looks like this.

```
Void setup () {

    // Put your setup code here

}

Void loop () {

    // Put your main code here

}
```

If, for whatever reason, you can't find the bare minimum file, you can easily type in the above code into the editor. I am sure this can be very confusing, but I will explain it to you now.

- **Void Setup** – This is a command that has been written into the IDE. This command only runs once when the program is run. It is here to ensure that it wipes any previously written code from memory, and it can start fresh with the new code.

22

- **Void Loop** – This is another command that has been written into the IDE. This command is run constantly until it reaches a command awaiting a response. This is where the core of the code will be written to do tasks.

- // - These are comment lines. When writing code, it is important that you write notes and keep sections properly documented. As your programs and your increase in size and complexity, notes will be your saving grace. Also, when we comment on our code, it will be much easier for others to understand what it was we were trying to develop. So, if you get nothing else out of this book, comment, comment, and comment on your code often.

- **{ and }** – These are your opening and closing brackets. When developing code in any language, the compiler will understand that { states that we are starting a specific section of code and that } closes that section of code. Look at it as the paragraph breaks in a book. Without them, the words would continue to ramble on.

With this skeleton and framework now on the screen, we are ready to take the next step and start writing our very first sketch.

Testing Communications

The next step is to ensure that we are communicating with the Arduino. To accomplish this, make sure that the Arduino is connected to the USB port from the previous step. Then in the IDE, go to the following.

```
Tools -> Port -> "Device"
```

Under the "Device," it should say what port number you are on and your device's name. If nothing is listed, unplug your device, wait for a second and plug it back in. If you see the device, make sure that there is a check mark next to the name. This tells the IDE that it is connected. If there is no check mark, simply hover the mouse over the device and click on it. If everything is good, move on to the next step.

```
Tools -> Boards -> "Your Board"
```

It is important that you ensure that the board that you are using is selected. If your board is not the correct one selected, you will experience problems or cause damage. Typically, the board you are using will automatically be detected, but if it is not, this is where you can change it.

That's it!

If you have made it this far, then you are ready to get started and work on your very first program. Congratulations!

Your First Program

This is where the fun begins. From this point, we are going to develop our very first program. Now, don't get too excited. In the world of programming and development, instructors will give the "Hello World" programming example. What this program does is show students or others who are looking to program a simple win.

It will cover some of the most basic commands you will ever use and give you the confidence to say "YES, I can do this!"

```
Blink | Arduino 1.8.5

Blink §

This example code is in the public domain.

http://www.arduino.cc/en/Tutorial/Blink
*/

// the setup function runs once when you press reset or power the board
void setup() {
  // initialize digital pin LED_BUILTIN as an output.
  pinMode(LED_BUILTIN, OUTPUT);
}

// the loop function runs over and over again forever
void loop() {$
  digitalWrite(LED_BUILTIN, HIGH);    // turn the LED on (HIGH is the voltage level)
  delay(1000);                        // wait for a second
  digitalWrite(LED_BUILTIN, LOW);     // turn the LED off by making the voltage LOW
  delay(1000);                        // wait for a second
}

32                                                    Arduino/Genuino Uno on COM1
```

In a typical program, the hello world example will look like this.

```
{

Print "Hello World";

}
```

When the application is compiled and run, the results will look like this on the screen

```
Hello World
```

Why is this done?

To put it simply, they do it to test that everything is working in your IDE and second, it is a rite of passage into the world of programming. Once you write this type of program, you will never do it again.

The Pin 13 Version of Hello World

On the Arduino, you will see a series of pins starting from zero and going all the way to thirteen. These are on the edge of your Arduino "uno" and others. These pins are open except for pin thirteen. Pin thirteen is connected to an LED that, when communicated with, it will blink.

This is our Hello World response. It is also the simplest build or application that we can make to show what the Arduino can do. Let's get started.

If you have followed along, you should have the bare minimum program open, and your device should be hooked up and communicating with your computer. If not, follow those steps before proceeding. Next, you want to place your cursor under the // and before the }. This will ensure that you are in the Void Setup section and can start writing code.

The command that we are going to use is called pinMode. This command will tell the Arduino that you wish to communicate with a specific pin or set of pins. When writing this command, make sure that you write it just as written since it is case-sensitive. Writing it like this, Pinmode, PinMode, pinmode, or any other variation will not work.

pinMode should now turn orange in color. If it does, then you did it correctly, and it should look like the code below.

```
Void setup ()   {

   // Put your setup code here

   pinMode

   }
```

The next step is to give the command some parameters. Parameters tell the command what you are working with and what you want to do with it. For this command, we need to give it two parameters, the pin and what the pin will be doing.

You want to add to the command on the same line where you have written pinMode. The task we want it to perform is to talk to pin 13 and use it as an output.

```
pinMode (13, OUTPUT);
```

When ending your command, you want to close it with the closing parentheses, and every command that is given ends with a semi-colon ';'. One of the most common mistakes in programming is forgetting to end your line with a ; (semicolon.) This should always be the first thing you check when receiving an error.

Now, it is time to decide what we want to do with pin 13. Since it is selected and ready to go, we can tell it to do something. The simplest thing that we can do in this example is turn on the light. We will do that in the next set of commands. Put your cursor into the void loop section to write your next set of commands.

```
}

Void loop ()   {

   // Put your main code here

}
```

In this command, we are going to use the digitalWrite command. Again, all commands we are writing are in camel case. This is because we can't start commands with a capital letter, and we can't have spaces. So, to help programmers read code better, we use camel case, which is programmed into the IDE to work.

The digitalWrite command also takes two parameters just like pinMode did. The parameters will be the pin and the action we want to perform. In this example, we want to turn the light on so we will use the HIGH command.

Your code should look like this.

```
}

Void loop ()   {

   // Put your main code here

digitalWrite(13, HIGH);

}
```

From this point, we have completed our first program and are ready to see it work. To do this, we need to compile the code and send it to the Arduino. To do this, you want to look at the top of your interface for an arrow. This will be the second button at the top of the page. To compile and see if the application is working, click that button with your mouse.

On your screen, you will see the green bar moving as it processes. Once that is completed, you will see a black box open with a lot of code and commands pop onto the screen. This is your compiling area where errors or other notifications are presented.

Once everything is completed, which will only take a few seconds, you should be able to look over at your Arduino and see that the light that is connected to pin 13 is now on. If not, look at your code and ensure it looks like this.

```
Void setup ()   {

    // Put your setup code here

pinMode (13, OUTPUT);

}

Void loop ()   {

    // Put your main code here

digitalWrite(13 ,HIGH);

}
```

That's it! You are now officially an Arduino programmer and have completed the "Hello World" equivalent. Sit and feel good about your accomplishment.

Okay, let's see what we can do next. How about turning the light off? To accomplish this, we don't have to reinvent the wheel. We simply need to change a single word in your program. To turn the light off, simply change HIGH to LOW.

```
digitalWrite(13, LOW);
```

You don't want to change any of the other code. Simply change HIGH to LOW. Once completed, click on the arrow button once more, and it will communicate with the Arduino turning off the light.

Now, you have written two programs controlling your device. This might seem like a simple task for some people, but it shows a very important principle in programming. If we can do this to turn on a light, what other things can we turn on and off?

Make the Light Blink

The next program we will do is try to make the light blink. To accomplish this, we will need to modify our code a little bit. Try this for yourself and see if you can get the light to blink.

```
Void setup ()   {

    // Put your setup code here

    pinMode (13, OUTPUT);
```

```
}

Void loop ()  {

  // Put your main code here

digitalWrite(13, HIGH);

digitalWrite(13, LOW);

}
```

Once again, compile the application and send it to the Arduino. What happened?

Introducing a Delay

If you have followed the directions above and you don't think your light blinked, you would be wrong. It did blink. The problem is that it blinks so fast that the human eye can't tell if it is on or off. Therefore we want to introduce a delay.

A delay is simply that. We want to have a delay between the light turning off and on again in the loop. To do this, we will be working in milliseconds. When working in milliseconds, it is important to understand that one second of time equals one thousand milliseconds. To write this, we would use 1000 for 1 second, 2000 for 2 seconds, and so on. In our code, we want to delay the light for one second. To accomplish this, we will use the following line of code.

```
delay(1000);
```

This code will set a delay for one second before executing the next line of code. If you would like to have a longer delay, increase the number. To insert this into our program, we will need to put a space after turning it on and after turning it off. Review the following code and make the appropriate changes in yours.

```
Void loop ()   {

    digitalWrite(13, HIGH);

    delay(1000);

    digitalWrite(13, LOW);

    delay(1000);

}
```

If your application is complete, compile and run. If you've done it correctly this time, your light should be blinking.

Review

Up to this point in this book, we have introduced you to the Arduino, and prepared your computer to communicate and interface with the device. We also wrote our first set of programs to see a result. If you have accomplished this, give yourself a pat on the back for a job well done. You have officially taken the first steps into creating some cool projects.

Homework

Before moving on to the next chapter, it is a good idea to play with what we have already done. For your homework, your task is to see how fast and how slow you can get the light to blink. You will do this by changing the number in the delay. You want to raise it, lower it and see what you can do.

Consider adding additional delays in the process to simulate listening to music or talking to you with light. Have some fun with the light and prepare to move on to the next chapter and lesson.

Chapter 3

Understanding Circuits
and How Electricity Works

At the start of the book, we introduced you to the Arduino and what is needed to get it up and running. Now that we have our basics down, we need to start using hardware and other tools to build something with the Arduino.

Circuits

In its most basic form, a circuit is a way for electricity to travel from one location to another, producing an output. So, for instance, a light switch controls a circuit. When we flip the light switch on, it connects the circuit together, allowing electricity to flow. When we flip the switch off in a different direction, it shuts off the flow of electricity, allowing the light to turn off.

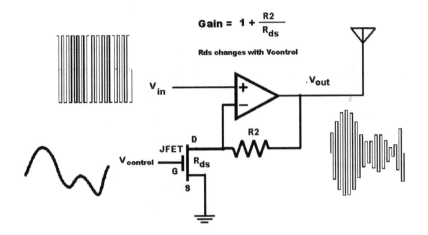

$$\text{Gain} = 1 + \frac{R2}{R_{ds}}$$

Rds changes with Vcontrol

A circuit has two basic states, on or off. When a circuit is on or open, electricity flows through, allowing the light or object to turn on. Off or closed is when we prevent the power from flowing to its destination.

Resisters

The next component will be the resister. The resister will be a buffer between the circuits to ensure that the power sent through into the device doesn't overload it or cause it to burn out. If we didn't have resisters in our circuits, then too much power could flow through.

The Breadboard

When working with the Arduino, we will use a lot of different components to help connect circuits to the device. The main component that will be holding all your LEDs and controls is known as the Bread Board.

When looking at the breadboard, you will see that there are rows and columns of holes. Down the center of the board, you will have some blank space that does not have any holes. This is known as the channel.

The breadboard works in connected columns. So, if you look at the board, you will see several long rows with other shorter columns. When connecting your devices up, they will go up and down in columns, not across in rows.

The space in the middle is known as the channel. This is where nothing will be set up and it is a buffer between either side of the breadboard. If you try to connect any components crossing over this channel, it will not work.

Cases and Chassis

As you start developing with Arduino you want to work with cases and chassis. These can be purchased commercially, or if you have a 3D printer, you can create your own base to connect your Arduino and Breadboard.

As you develop your skills, you will quickly find that you will want to have something that is easy to work with. Having wires running everywhere can quickly become messy and will be hard to fix problems later on. As a developer, considering wire management will take you a long way.

Positive and Negative Charge

When working with electricity, it is also very important that you understand that you are working with three components. The first is a positive charge, the second is a negative charge, and the third is the ground. When connecting items up to your breadboard, it is very important that you don't connect things wrong because positive and negative connections will cancel each other out and, in some cases, cause damage to your board, components, and Arduino.

Specialty Rows

When looking at your Arduino, you will see two special rows at the top of the breadboard and two special rows at the bottom of the breadboard. These rows will have either the plus + symbol or the − negative symbol. These rows are all connected, but the columns are not. So, you can connect going down the row of − negative connections or across with the + positive connections. These give you added power for ground and other needs for connecting to your Arduino.

Project #1 – Connecting an LED to Your Breadboard

Now that we have the basics, we will go into a quick project using the components and understanding how a circuit works to create our next project, which will be turning on an LED light.

What Is an LED light?

An LED light is a light that is more efficient than a traditional light bulb. In a traditional light bulb, we are heating up wires to the point that they are white hot. This white-hot wire will then illuminate light into a room, brightening it up.

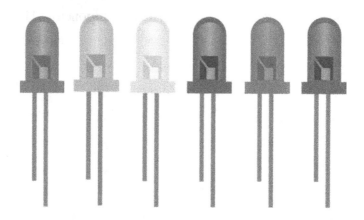

An LED light doesn't generate heat. We can use a more efficient light source in our projects. LED lights are starting to take over as replacements for the standard light bulb because they are easier to use, and they don't heat up. We can also control the power that is delivered to them, allowing us to do a lot more with light than we have ever done before. One example of this is Christmas Lights used in yard displays. Since we can control these lights, we can have them blink, change colors, and so much more. As you get better with the Arduino, you can create your own Christmas Light Display program and wow your neighbors.

Power Management

Another skill that you will want to learn is power management. As we add more and more components to our Arduino and our project, understand that each item will draw more and more power. You want to ensure that you are using resisters and other devices to take up the power consumption. If you tax your Arduino too hard with power, it can quickly burn out or have issues.

What Do We Need for This Project?

To start this project, you may want to look for a kit with many different components that you can play with. These kits are usually inexpensive and will give you more components than what we will go over here in this example.

330 OHM Resister

The first component that we will need is a resister. The one for this project will be a 330 OHM, which basically means that it has a charge or power rating of 0.25 Watt. When looking at this resister, it will be orange or tan in color.

LED

The next component that you will need is an LED. The LEDs will usually come in a packet of different colors. For this project, take out a RED LED to use. If you don't have a RED LED, that is fine, you can pick any color that you want.

Wires

You will want to take some wires out of your kit and put them to the side. The wires will connect all the components through the breadboard, making our components work together and complete the circuit.

Building Your Project

Now that we have all of the components that we need, let's jump in and do a quick review and get started.

We need to have the Arduino hooked up to your computer. We need to have your resister, LED, and wires ready to go. If you are set, let's start building.

First Step

The first step in the project is to connect the Arduino to the breadboard. If you recall from the first couple of chapters and the first lesson, we can do this by connecting to pin 13.

Carefully, take one end of a wire and connect it to pin 13 on the Arduino. You may need to get a magnifying glass to see it if you have bad vision. Take your time and ensure that you are connecting to this pin since it can easily be missed.

Once connected to the Arduino, go ahead and connect the other end of the wire to any random column on the breadboard. This will connect the Arduino to the breadboard. Now, the next step is to connect the resister.

Connecting the Resister

On the breadboard, look at the column you have the wire connected to. You want to connect one end of the resister into the hole right underneath the wire in the same column. You will then take the other end of the resister and connect it to another hole in a different column.

Connecting the LED

The next step in the project is to connect the LED to the breadboard. When you are looking at the LED, you will see that one leg is longer than the other. The longer leg of the LED is the positive end of the LED, and the shorter is negative. When you hook up this LED to the resister, make sure you hook up the positive end to the resister and the negative away from the resister.

Take the long end and plug it into the same column that you have the resister plugged into, and then the short end goes into a separate column.

Connecting to Ground

The next step is to connect everything together, and to do this, we need another wire that we will connect to the ground. To do this, look at your Arduino and right next to pin 13, you will see a pin that says GND, which stands for ground.

Take one end of your wire and hook it into that pin. You want to leave the other end of the wire unhooked at the moment; we will connect it after we have written our program. To do that, review the steps in the first chapter and load the Bare Minimum program. Once there, we are going to write the following program.

Writing the Code

The code for this application is going to be almost the same as the code we wrote in the previous application. In fact, you can probably use the same application with a few changes. Review the code below, write it into your application and upload it to the Arduino.

```
Void Setup Code - Write the following under
the void setup code

    pinMode(13, OUTPUT);



Void Loop code - Write the following under
the void loop code

    digitalWrite(13 ,HIGH);

    delay(500);

    digitalWrite(13, LOW);

    delay(500);
```

This code is designed to turn the LED light on, wait for half a second, turn the light off, wait for a half second and then turn it on again. Your next step is to upload the program to the Arduino.

Once uploaded, you will see that nothing has happened. This is because we have not connected the ground wire to the bard completing the circuit. To do this take the other end of the ground wire and connect it to the same column that you have the short end of the LED hooked into. Once connected, the program will execute, and you will see the LED light turn on, wait, then turn off.

If your LED isn't working properly, make sure that you have everything connected to the proper areas of the breadboard and that you are connected to the correct pin on the Arduino.

Adding and Switching Up Pins

Now that you have successfully completed your first project using the breadboard and the Arduino, it is time to start switching things up and take your current project to the next level.

When looking at your Arduino, you will see that you have up to 13 pins that you can work with. So far, we have been working with only pin 13, but we have others that we can use. For your next part of the project, unhook the wire that you have connected to pin 13 and connect it to pin 8. Once you unhook that wire from the pin and connect it to another pin, it will stop working.

Go ahead and connect that same wire back to pin 13. You will now see that your program is running, and the LED is blinking again. In the next step of the project, we are going to connect the LED to pin 8.

Reconnect that wire back to Pin 8 and go into your code. We need to change the code so that the Arduino knows that we are working with another pin configuration. Go in and change 13 to 8 everywhere in your code. Once completed, reupload the code to the Arduino.

When the code becomes active, you will see the LED blinking again. This exercise aims to show you that you can add and move different pins around. This will allow you to add additional components and do different commands with these components. This is the power of programming.

Your code should look like this now.

Void Setup Code – write the following under the void setup code

```
pinMode(8, OUTPUT);
```

```
Void Loop code - write the following under
the void loop code

digitalWrite(8, HIGH);

delay(500);

digitalWrite(8, LOW);

delay(500);
```

Controlling the Blinking of the LED

Similar to what we did in our first project where we controlled the light on the Arduino, we will do the same for the LED. You want to go into your code and change the 500 to different numbers, which will be your delay. The way you do this is explained in the second chapter.

See what you can get the LED to do before going on and adding additional LEDs.

Connect Multiple LED Lights to the Board

For the next project, we are going to connect multiple LED lights to the board, and we are going to have them all do different things. This should be simple if you have successfully gotten one of the lights to work. For this project, you will need the following components.

- 2 more 330 OHM resisters

- 2 more LED's

- 2 more wires to connect from the pins to the board

Once you have all of these components, go ahead and connect them to the breadboard in the same fashion you did the first LED. Remember that columns work together to form connections. Once you have the connections created on the breadboard, you want to go into the code and copy what you did previously, changing the pin numbers and the delays. Upload your finished code to the Arduino and see what you can make happen.

Chapter 4

Working with Variables

Congratulations on getting to this point in the training. You should feel very proud of yourself for what you have accomplished. For some of you just turning on lights isn't that exciting, but it does prove a concept in development. Just think of connecting fans, GPSs, Robot arms, and anything else you can imagine. When working on these simple projects, don't think of it as simple; consider it developing strong foundations. Now that you can control the light, you can control anything.

Understanding Variables

Now that we have developed the foundation and have completed a few projects, it is time to start making these projects more complicated. The way that we can do this is by introducing variables into our programs.

What Is a Variable?

In its simplest form, a variable is a name. We use variables in programming all the time to identify a specific item or set of items in our code. Variables can also work together to have a simple or complex logic to them. We can make a variable be true or we can make it be false. Depending on the state that it is in, it will dictate what actions are taken in the program.

When working with programming, it is vital that you understand variables and how they work. They will make working with your code and changing things much easier. Let's look at how complicated a program could become if we hardcoded numbers into our program.

Types of Variables

In our program, we are going to start working with two types of variables. These are going to be Integers and Floats.

- **Integers** – When working with integers, we are working with whole numbers. This is 0 – 9999999999 and beyond. For the content in this book, we will be working with whole numbers.

- **Floats** – Floats are all the numbers in between the whole numbers. So, for example 3.14 would be the float for PI. It is very important that you know what type of variable you are working with; otherwise, the program will not work or it will give you an unexpected result.

Naming Variables

When we name a variable, we really have a lot of control over what we name them. This will help in referencing back to something later in our code. One of the main things you need to understand is that variables are case-sensitive. This means that the variable names, balloon and Balloon and BallOon, represent different variables.

Naming Conventions

When writing programs, it is important that you create and stick to a standard naming convention. What this means is that you want to pick a specific way you name your variables and stick to it throughout your program. One of the best ways of doing this is through camel case.

The variables you want to write should be like this variableName. As you can see, we start with a lowercase letter and then the second word in our variable is uppercase. This is how you want to create your variables. This will also help if you hand off your code to others since this is a standard convention.

Never Start with Numbers or Underscores

Another thing that some people may want to do is start a variable with a number or an underscore. Starting with a number such as 1variableName won't work. It will throw an error in your code. Also, starting with an underscore _variableName will also become confusing and give errors.

When creating your variables, simply use this style variableName, and you will not have problems.

Use Variables for Anything That Can Change in Your Code

The main reason that you will use variables in your code is to make changing things much easier. When we create a variable, we simply insert that variable everywhere we want to represent that information. Here is an example of a nightmare code that we will have to deal with if we don't use variables.

```
Void Setup
  pinMode(8, OUTPUT);
Void Loop code
  digitalWrite(8, HIGH);
delay(500);
digitalWrite(8, LOW);
delay(500);
```

When looking at this code, you might think that it is too simple to become complicated. Well, you are wrong. This code can become very complicated and time-consuming if you don't use variables. If you did your homework and added additional pins and LED lights, then you could have tons of these lines of code referring back to different things.

Think of it like this, what if a pin on your board stopped working for some reason? You would have to go back into your code, find all Pin 8s and change 8 to 13 or 12 or to whatever you need. What do you think would happen if you missed an 8 or accidentally changed it to a 7?

When working with code, we want to make things simple and modular. We want to have a specific set of variables to simply change one parameter, which will affect the entire program. So how do we do this?

Above the void setup, we will want to start writing our variables. We start our variables above the void setup because we want these variables to be read first, ensuring that they are written into memory and can be executed by the rest of the program. If we don't do it here, we can't declare them, and they can't be used.

How Do We Write a Variable?

Writing a variable is very easy. The first thing we need to do is declare what type of variable it is. Since we are going to be working with numbers, we will be using Integers. The way we declare an integer is with the code INT.

```
INT myPin=8;
```

```
Void Setup
```

As you can see, the variable is above everything else in our code and has a specific name of myPin. Now, everywhere we want to work with this specific pin, we will use myPin.

What if we wanted to use pin 13 instead of 8? It is simple, you would go into the variable and change the 8 to a 13, and your program will work. Well, once we insert the variables. Simply declaring a variable isn't good enough to get it to work. We need to actually use the variable in our code. To do this, we need to change everywhere the number 8 or 13 appears in the myPin variable.

```
Void Setup

  pinMode(myPin, OUTPUT);

Void Loop code

  digitalWrite(myPin, HIGH);

delay(500);

digitalWrite(myPin, LOW);

delay(500);
```

Now, compile and send up to the Arduino. If you haven't changed anything else in your program, it should work as if you had the 8 hard-coded into the program.

What Else Can We Change with Variables?

We can change anything that we want to if we declare it. For instance, if we want to change the delays in the blinking, we can create a variable for that. Here is how we would do that.

```
INT blinkOn(500);

INT blinkOff(1000);
```

In this example, we can use a single blink variable if we want to, but adding multiple variables allows us to change up the blink if we want to. Here is how the code will work now.

```
Void Setup

    pinMode(myPin, OUTPUT);

Void Loop code

    digitalWrite(myPin ,HIGH);

delay(blinkOn);

digitalWrite(myPin, LOW);

delay(blinkOn);
```

This will keep the light blinking on and off at a constant rate. However, if you want to change things up and have a different delay, you can now simply change the variables.

```
Void Setup

    pinMode(myPin, OUTPUT);
```

```
Void Loop code

    digitalWrite(myPin, HIGH);

delay(blinkOn);

digitalWrite(myPin, LOW);

delay(blinkOff);
```

All you have to do now is simply change the numbers in the variables to change the delay speeds. You can also add additional variables to your program as well if you want to add additional functions to your program. Here is an example. Code it and see what you get.

```
INT blinkOn(500);

INT blinkOff(1000);

INT rapidBlink(100);

INT longPauseBlink(10000);
```

Go ahead and add the above variables to your code and then add additional delays to your program and insert the variables. You can then have some fun and see how you can make the LED blink.

Challenge

Here is your challenge for this chapter. Go and add in 3 LED lights with your resisters and wires. Have a red LED, a green LED, and a yellow LED. Then in your code, do the following.

```
INT redLED=8;
```

```
INT yellowLED=10;

INT greenLED=13;

INT blinkRed=(500);

INT blinkYellow=(500);

INT blinkGreen=(500);

INT myDelay=(500);
```

Put these variables into your code and do a traffic light type situation. You want the red light to come on and delay for a few seconds, then have the green light come on so the cars can go, then have the yellow turn on before changing to red again. You should have all the code written for you above; it is simply a matter of expanding on it to create the specific situation. Follow the logic of the program and see what you can make happen.

When you understand what variables are and how they work, you can start to create some interesting and more complex applications. In this chapter, we introduced you to simple variables. However, we will explore many more variables in this book. Once you get a variable declared and inserted into your code, changing a single line of code can have your application doing amazing things.

Chapter 5

analogWrite -
Controlling Your Brightness Levels

S o far in this book we have been working with digital signals and the code for digitalWrite. In our examples, we have used digitalWrite to turn lights and LED's on and off. But what if we wanted to control the intensity of the lights we are working with? What if we wanted to have a real dim light, a medium brightness to our light, and a really bright light?

With the code digitalWrite, we only had two states that the light could be in. On or HIGH or off LOW. When we introduce you to analogWrite, we are introducing you to a way control the brightness or voltage that you are sending to our LEDs.

What Does Analog Do?

When working with analog, we are working with numbers. This gives us more power to control how much power or voltage is being sent to your LED or other connected devices. When working with analog, we are working with numbers between 0 and 255. The number 0 would represent LOW in our code, and 255 would represent HIGH.

To work with the amount of power and light an LED has, using analogWrite will allow us to do different things. Instead of turning the lights on or off, we can change how bright they are. Here is how it will work.

Setting up the Board

The first step in the process is setting up the board. Unlike when digitalWrite could use pins 2 – 13, with analogWrite, we can only use specific pins that have the mark above the number. On your Arduino board, these pins will be 3, 5, 6, 9, 10, and 11. All the other pins won't work with this example.

Knowing Your Numbers

The next thing that you need to understand is that you can control the power of the light by using the numbers 0 – 255. In the analog world, you have 256 numbers to work with. We start counting at 0, which gives us a total of 255. The higher the number we set in our variable, the brighter the lights will be.

Setting up the Board

Now that you understand the basics, let's have some fun and actually start building the board. For this example, let's make it simple and use pin 9. You can use any of the other pins listed, but if we work with pin 9, we know it will work.

We want to set up our board the same way we have been throughout the book so far. You should already be set up if you haven't changed your board much throughout the lessons. However, if you are not, you will want the 1 LED, the wire you will insert into pin 9, the ground wire, and your resister.

Go back to the first lesson, where we set up the board and complete those steps. Once set up, we will be able to jump into the programming.

Setting up the Variables

The first thing we always want to do from this point forward is set up our variables. We want to work with variables so we have the power to make changes quickly and don't have to mess with the code.

The first variable we need to set up is for our pin. To do this, write the following code.

```
Int redPin=9;
```

This will give the pin the variable of redPin, and we are telling it that it's using pin 9. You can change the number if you have used another pin slot.

Write the Code

Now that the variable is declared, we can start writing code. To start, write the following line of code.

```
Void Setup

   pinMode(redPin, OUTPUT);



Void loop

   analogWrite(redPin, 255);
```

Now, we will improve on this in the next step, but go ahead and compile and run. If everything has worked correctly, the light should now be on.

Controlling the Voltage

If everything worked, you should have your light on. This means everything is working correctly, and we can start controlling the voltage. As stated, we can work with numbers from 0 to 255. 0 will correspond to 0 or off, and 255 will correspond to 5 volts. If we were to change the 255 to 120 and run the application, the LED would now be dim or half as bright. Go ahead and change the 255 to a smaller number, compile and run.

If everything is correct, you would have dimmed the light on the LED. Pretty cool.

The next thing that we want to do is add a variable so we can control this dynamically. To do this, go ahead and create a variable and call it bright.

```
INT = bright(255);
```

Now, let's change the code we wrote in the previous example and change the 255 to the bright variable. It should look like this.

```
Void loop

analogWrite(redPin, bright);
```

Go ahead and run the application again, and you will see no change in the brightness of the light, but the light will still be on at full intensity. To control the light, you can now easily just change that 255 to a new number and run the code again, affecting the brightness of the LED.

Playing with What We Have Learned So Far

Before we can move on to more complicated builds, it is important that you understand what we have gone through so far and what you can do. To recap everything, we are working with a voltage that, when sent through the Arduino, will go through wires connected to a breadboard. This breadboard will create a circuit that will do a specific task.

On the breadboard, we are using resistors, LEDs and wires. When connecting them correctly, we are building a circuit that we can control with the code. With this basic understanding, we then moved on to controlling the brightness of the lights that we used. On the surface, this might not seem like a lot, but we now have the foundation and understanding in the scope of making things work.

Chapter 6

Exploring Coding

U p to this point in your education, we have gone over the very basics of what your Arduino can do. But how can we make it do more complex actions that can really give us real-world applications? This is done through coding. Now, I said that there wasn't a lot of coding involved in the Arduino, and that is true, you can use basic commands that we have done so far to create light displays and interactions with your environment, but if you really want to harness the power of your device, it is important to learn to code.

Look for Prewritten Code

Earlier in this book, I mentioned that a lot of the code that you will write for your projects has already been written and commented on. You can search on Google for Arduino Code or Arduino Libraries and you will find a massive collection of prewritten code that is free to use.

As you develop code and start creating programs, these code libraries and snippets will go a long with in not only making your project develop faster, but you can add in features, functions, and more that you never thought possible. Also, you want to look at this code to learn and understand how it was written and what it does. The more you can educate yourself, the more you can do in a shorter time.

How Do We Code?

One of the nice things about the Arduino is that it is open source. This means that anyone can create devices and code that can be used to do specific projects. These are often given away on GitHub or another software platform for people to download and modify. There are some places that may have more complex code or projects that work for specific tasks that may charge, but for the most part, you can get code for free.

You can code in the Arduino language like we have been doing so far in this book or you can code in different languages such as Python, C++, and others. We will talk more about those later in the book. However, I just wanted you to know that you have a lot of options when it comes to programming.

With that said, let's get into the core understanding of how programs work and the structure you will use in every language you may program in, whether it is for the Arduino or not.

Include

The Include command is more of an advanced command that will allow you to connect specific files that you may have been developing into a single program. For example, if you have a file filled with all of your variables. This would look something like this.

```
INT   redLED(255);

INT blueLED(122);

INT blueLED122(110);

Delay500(500);
```

All of these would be in a single file. You would add the include function above all other lines of code. For example, it would be like this, include Variables. This would now connect the variables file to your application, and you could start pulling the variables you have written into that file. This is a great way to really keep your code modular. The more code you can break into different files and connect them, the faster you can develop applications since you have already done all the hard work.

Operators

When working with code, you will want to do a lot of math. To accomplish this, you will want to use operators. When working with operators, we can also create dynamic code when we use variables. So, for example, if we wanted to change the rate at which an LED blinked, we can do this by setting up variables and operators.

- Add +

- Subtract –

- Multiply *

- Divide /

- Equals = or ==

The == checks to see if both numbers on either side of the equals are the same. So if

```
redLED == blueLED then greenLED(600);
```

This would check to see if the red LED light and the blue LED light had the same numbers. If they did, then the green LED light would blink. If not, the green LED wouldn't blink.

- Remainder %

- != Not equal to –

This will be used if you want to compare two numbers and determine if they are not equal to each other or a specific number. For example, if

```
redLED != blueLED then greenLED(1000);
```

This starts to get into loops which we will talk about soon.

- Less than > – This checks to see if a number is less than another number

- Greater than < - This checks to see if a number is greater than another number.

- Input – We talked about this previously in the book. When we use Input, we are expecting something to be put into the Arduino.

- Output – This is the opposite of input. We expect to get something out of the Arduino when we use this.

- **INPUT_PULLUP** – This is the code that you would use when programming a button.

- **VOID** – This function is used when we don't want the Arduino to expect any type of input from the setup. So, we use this at the beginning of our programs for Void Setup and Void Loop.

- **Boolean** – A Boolean is a placeholder for either when an event is True or False. That is all it is used for.

- **Byte** – This is used to work with 8-bit systems and characters from 0 to 255. We talked about this prior in the book in our last example.

- **Integer** – Similar to the Byte command, which is 8-bit, an integer is 16-bit and can hold numbers from -32,768 to 32,767. If you are looking for even more numbers to work with for whatever reason, you can upgrade to a 32-bit board with the Arduino Duo and have numbers between -2,147,483,648 to 2,147,483,647.

- **Long** – If you are working with really long numbers and the Integer won't work for you, it is possible to use the Long command. With this you can have numbers from -2,147,483,648 to 2,147,483,647

- **Float** – When we want to have more precise numbers, we will want to use a float. A float will allow you to have up to 6 or 7 decimal places. These decimal places will then be multiplied by ten to the power of a maximum of 38. This means that you can have very complex and precise numbers in your calculations.

If Statements

Now we are going to get into more logic of programming. With If statements we are working on understanding if something happens. For example,

```
IF redLED = (500);
```

This is setting the condition to do something if , but what if

66

```
redLED = (500)
```

What do we do from here?

Then Statements

The Then Statement will tell the IF statement what to do if true. For example,

```
IF redLED = (500) then greenLED = (1000);
```

These two statements will be used to create conditions that will allow you to do more advanced programming with your Arduino. You can also create a series of options with the Else Statement.

Else Statement

The Else Statement states that if condition statement one is not true and statement two isn't true, do this. Here is an example.

```
If redLED = (500);

Then Delay(1000);

Else

  Delay(2000);
```

How this read is if the LED light variable is equal to 500, then we want to delay the cycle for 1 second, which is 1000. If we change the variable for redLED to anything other than 500, then we will delay for 2 seconds which is 2000.

Now you can see how important variables are. If we want to make the condition true or false, we need to have something to change it at will.

Arrays

The next concept that I want to go over is arrays. Arrays allow us to store specific data into a specific variable. For example, if we want to store a collection of pins on the board, we could do this with an array.

When working with an array, we can keep our data clean and can connect to code with less typing. Here is an example.

If we were to create an array for pins on the board, we would first have to give the array a name.

```
Name - LEDPins
```

From there, we need to define the scope. When working with an array, understand that indexing is zero-based. This means that the first element in the array is at index 0, the second is at index 1, and so on. So, if you had 6 elements, the final one would be defined as LEDPins[5].

Next, we have to define what is being stored in the array. This is what will be pulled from the array when we connect with the code. In other applications, we can use data such as names. You would type each name in your array with a comma next to it.

```
John, Beth, Mark, Eric, Chris
```

The code you save in the array must be enclosed with brackets. { }; For our example, we will not hold names but pins. So, this is how the code would look.

```
Name LEDPins[5] = {4,6,7,8,9,13};
```

As you can see, we put in the number 5, but we actually have 6 numbers. This is how we define an array that can be used anywhere in our applications. So why is this useful?

This is useful because now we have a container that we can easily pull a pin from and use. If we didn't have arrays, we would have to code each pin individually with a variable, and that can get messy quickly.

This is the foundation for programming. When you look at all of this, your head might start spinning; however, it is basic but very powerful. When we learn how these components work together, we can create anything that is simple to extremely complex. If you can dream it, you can make it with the Arduino and some basic code.

Chapter 7

Building off the Basics

Now that we understand what the Arduino is, how it can be assembled, and what types of programming we need to make things happen, we will dive in and look at an assortment of different components you can add to the board to make cool stuff happen.

Kits

The first thing that you really want to do is investigate different kits that are available. When working with kits, we are given all the components needed to complete a set number of different projects. These kits can also be interchangeable with other components to take simple projects to the next level.

As you explore kits, you will want to take note of the components inside. Each of these components will need code to run. To ensure that you have good code, you want to do a search for libraries. Go into Google and type in the name of the component and libraries. You will then find different code to help you properly run the component.

Shields

The first component that you want to look into is shields. With shields, you are given extra connectivity and features that can't be installed on your baseboard. With your shields, you can have added functionality such as wireless internet connectivity, store data obtained from web and other sensors, male and female connectors to add additional traditional devices, and so much more. You can choose from a wide range of shields, and when connecting them together, you have limitless possibilities.

Header Strips

If you are looking to expand your current board, you can look into getting different header strips. These header strips can be installed onto your existing board, allowing you to have more pin connections to connect up different devices. These header stripes work on the Uno and other boards. Make sure that when purchasing, they will work on your specific board.

Thumb Joystick

A cool device you can get is the thumb joystick. This can be used to help move current in different directions in your projects. If you move it to the left, the left LED lights could light up. Another great feature is that it's analog which means you can measure your movements in 8-bit. This is good if you want to have a certain number of lights turn on when it hits a specific voltage or something similar.

Mini MP3 Player

When you want to create something cool, you might consider the mini MP3 Player. This will allow you to program music and have it play out of a connected device.

Raspberry Pi to Arduino MKR bridge HAT

If you have been working with other devices, you may want to try to connect them to your Arduino. Another popular device is the Raspberry Pi. If you have been working with them, you can get this bridge adaptor kit to help connect the two devices together to make something better. This is a more advanced piece of hardware that will need soldering, so it shouldn't be on the list of a newbie. Just know that you have the power to connect them together.

Dipole Pentaband Waterproof Antenna

You might want to use this cool device as a wireless access point. When you connect the device to your Arduino, you have the power to access wi-fi signals and online networks.

Buzzers

You can connect an assortment of different buzzers to your device. These buzzers will hum and vibrate according to the amount of voltage and current that is being sent to them. You can connect these to other devices, which can be used for communication and other projects.

RGB Color Sensor

This is a sensor that, when attached to your device, can detect the different Red, Green, and Blue you have in a specific color.

Heart Rate Monitor Sensor

This can be used to create a health device. You can connect it to check your blood pressure and heart rate. Some people will use this device to create a love tester.

Digital Shake Sensor

With this sensor, you have the ability to create a device that can sense movement or motion. Connect this to LEDs and you can have different lights show up if something is moving at a specific speed. One idea for this project would be to create something that had a green, yellow and red LED. Connect the sensor to the board and program it to turn on the green when there is very little motion and yellow when you are moving too quickly or the device is above your initial parameters. Finally, you can have it turn red when you have gone too far. This can be a great game to see if you can make it through an obstacle course or other hazards.

Analog LM35 Temperature Sensor

Measuring heat and temperature can be a great project for you to work on, and there are so many different options that you can test the heat on you are limitless. One idea is to monitor the heat in your pet's cage. If you have a lizard or turtle, you will want to make sure that the temperature is constant. With the heat sensor, you can easily connect to your lamp, turning up or down the voltage, so the light gets brighter or darker according to the specific temperature you want the cage to be.

Analog Sound Sensor for Arduino

Next to light, you can also test and see how sound is monitored with your device. If your parents tell you that the television is too loud or perhaps you are playing your music too loud, you can create a sensor and LED lights that will notify you when it is too loud. You can also use the same technology to alert you when your parents or someone is walking toward your room. If someone gets too close to your door, the music is automatically turned down and then goes back up when they leave.

Analog Carbon Monoxide Sensor (MQ7)

If you are working in a factory or if you are working somewhere where carbon monoxide could be present, creating one of these sensors could be a lifesaver. Since carbon monoxide is odorless and tasteless, the only way to protect yourself is with this sensor.

Digital Infrared Motion Sensor

In our previous example, we talked about detecting if someone is coming close to your room while you are playing music. With the digital inferred motion sensor, you can set this up outside your room or down a hall that no one would walk down unless they were going to your room. Once this sensor is tripped, you can have your Arduino lower the volume on your stereo or do other actions like turn on and off your lights in the room.

Analog Soil Moisture Sensor

If you are into gardening or working with plants, then this sensor could be a great help for you. Think about creating an automatic watering system that turns on a hydroponics system to water your plants. Or, on a simpler scale, have a motor attached to a panel that allows water to drip out of a water source. When the moisture sensor doesn't detect the right amount of moisture in the soil, it turns on and allows water to fill your plants. Once the sensor detects that the soil is moist enough, it will turn off and stop the water from flowing.

Digital Speaker Module

This speaker can be used in our previous listing of the MP3 Player. You can connect the speaker module to your board and send signals that can beep or play noise. If you have the mp3 device hooked up, you can take your MP3 music and play it through your Arduino.

130 DC Motor Module

If you want to make things move, you will need to have a motor. This DC Motor is a small motor that will allow you to connect other devices to it, allowing them to move. If you are looking to do the watering example stated above, you can use this to open the gate that is holding the water back and then, when done, have the motor go in the opposite direction to close everything up again.

12V 2A American Standard AC/DC Power Adaptor

After you are done downloading the software to your Arduino, you may want to disconnect the device from your computer. You can do this by getting a power adaptor. This power adaptor will allow you to move your creation, and have a steady power source, and since the program is already stored on your device, you no longer need it connected unless you are downloading new instructions and programming.

Analog Voltage Divider

You will want to use a voltage divider when you need to move different volts to different devices or items on your board. How this works is you can control the amount of voltage going to any device. The good thing about this is that you can't divide more than twenty-five volts in total.

Wearable Sensors and Lights

When trying to come up with different projects to show off your skills and what you have learned so far in this book, you might want to impress your friends by doing something with wearable lights and sensors. You can get what is known as a light-up tee shirt kit. With this kit, you have different lights and sensors that you can program with your Arduino. You can then take those and sew them into your clothing, so when you walk around, they light up, blink and do different things depending on your specific situation.

These wearable kits come with a battery pack that will supply them with power, and once programmed, they store the code in memory. These items are cool for people who want to step outside the box and really take some basic skills to the next level.

When it comes to the Arduino, there are a lot of different things you can set up to occur. You can allow your imagination to run wild with additional tools, boards, shields, and accessories. Many applications and programs that you create can have a useful purpose in the real world. However, being creative and learning how things work will take your skills to a new level.

Chapter 8

Introduction to Python

S o far in this book, we have been using the native Arduino environment to write the source code for our projects. As you progress with your programming and your development skills, you can also go into other languages to program your board. With these other languages, you may have more control and even more prewritten applications that will work with your device.

Since you are a beginner, we won't dive too deep into Python, but it should be something that we touch upon simply because it is an option that might be easier for people to use.

You will want to visit this website to learn about Python as a programming language. https://pypi.org/

Repositories

When working with Python, you will also be working with repositories. These are going to be code examples and full applications that are freely given to the community to use, modify and learn from.

To find the current listing of projects related to the Arduino, you can visit the link above and do a search or use the following link.

https://pypi.org/search/?q=Arduino&o=

Here are some projects listed that you can download and install.

- A Python API to control Arduino boards.
- A Python project to test the health of your board
- C Classes to help manage and work with Arrays
- Program to control lights on your Arduino
- Programs to help validate data
- Readout software for temperature sensors

- Libraries to help communicate between different Arduino boards

And so much more.

When working with your Arduino, it is a good idea to find what others have done, look at their code and see it in action. Once you are working with something that runs properly, you can easily go in and make changes to see what you can do to improve them.

Getting Python

Python is an open-source programming language which means it is free and developed by a core group of people. Since the application is open source, you can get it for almost all operating systems such as Windows, macOS, and Linux.

You can visit the following website - https://www.python.org/ to get your copy of Python.

Python vs. Arduino Code

In the previous chapters, we introduced you to the different coding that you can do with Arduino. In this chapter, we will show you what you can do with Python and how it differs from Arduino.

Commenting Code

The first thing you want to learn is how to comment your code. Any good programmer will spend a lot of time making comments and notes in their code so that when they revisit the application or hand it off to another developer, they know what was going on and don't have to try and figure it out.

When you are commenting in Arduino, you will use the // marks to indicate where your comment was started. With Python, you can use the # symbol to indicate where you want to start a comment.

```
# This is a comment in Python

// This is a comment in Arduino Code
```

Variables

In all programming languages, you will have variables. These will allow you to collect and store information generated by your application and used later. When working with the Arduino, you would have to declare your variables first. This means that in the Void Start() section of code, you would have to list all of the variables used in the application.

In Python, you have non-declarable variables. This means that you can declare a variable anywhere in your code that you want, and it will be used as soon as you declare it. This can make programming a little more robust since if you need to have a variable for a specific action, you can simply create it and not have to drag yourself through your code to the beginning and write it.

A drawback to this is that you may start to get confused about what you have set up for variables. Since they don't have to be in a specific location, trying to remember if you have declared it, used it, or what it is used can become an issue.

Here is an example

```
X = 5
```

```
Y = 8

Print x + y
```

This code can appear anywhere you need it in your code.

Casting Variables

If you want to define the type of variable in your code, it is known as casting. To do this, you would write your code as you did in the Arduino.

```
X = str("The boy is here") - This is for a
string

Y = int(55) - This is for an integer

Z = float(3) - This will read 3.0
```

Declaring Strings

You will need to declare a string using the double quotes in Arduino. " "

In Python, you can declare a string with either the double quotes " "

or the single quotes ' '

Case Sensitive

Both in the Arduino and Python language, all variables are case-sensitive. So, you would write redButton the same way in either language. Also, you want to set up your best programming practices and stay with them. They will serve you well in other languages.

Naming Variables

When naming your variables in Python, you can use any of the following methods:

- Use the underscore to start, i.e., _variableName

- Use all lowercase letters, i.e., variablename

- Use Camel Case, i.e., variableName

- Have an underscore in the name, i.e., variable_name

- Include a number, i.e., variableName2

You never want to start your variable with a number or have spaces in your variables. The best way to write a variable in any language is in camel case. Start your variable with a lowercase letter, have an uppercase letter for the middle, and nothing else. This way, you will always be consistent in your programming, and code can be translated into different languages.

As you can see, for the most part, the languages are pretty much the same. This gives programmers and developers a lot of freedom and flexibility when it comes to writing software applications for the web, operating systems, and hardware. Learning skills in whichever language you feel comfortable with will allow you to develop software faster and more efficiently.

Once you have written your application, it will be time to upload the script to your Arduino.

Compiling Python to Arduino

If you are going to use Python to program your boards, it is important to understand that some additional steps will be needed to upload the code to your board. What you want to do is visit the following website to get the full step-by-step instructions.

https://docs.arduino.cc/learn/programming/arduino-and-python

MicroPython

To transfer code to the Arduino, you will want to do your developing in an application known as MicroPython. This is application is similar to the Arduino development environment but specifically coded to write Python code for Arduino.

If you want to explore Python, you will need to have one of the following boards that support the MicroPython application. These boards are the Nano 33 BLE, Nano 33 BLE Sense, Nano RP2040 Connect, and the Portenta H7.

If you are a programmer who is currently using Python for other applications, then incorporating it into your Arduino can take your development skills to the next level. However, if you are just starting out, we suggest staying away from the other languages and continuing to use the IDE. Just know it is there if you want to start advancing your skills.

Using C++

Next to Python, you can also code in C++. This is almost exactly the same code but with some slight differences. When looking at different programming languages, take note of how easy it is for you to understand how they work. Then, as you start developing, pick a specific language.

Mixing and matching code

As you develop, you will find that you may be using C++ for some projects, Python for others, and even the IDE. As you find different libraries, you will also discover that people might use different languages to develop. Since the Arduino is open-source, all of these different languages and components will work together since the Arduino compiles everything down into its own useable language. So, feel free to experiment and have fun writing code.

Chapter 9

Using Libraries with the Arduino Programming IDE

What Is a Library in Programming?

The Arduino is not just a programming language; it's a framework that allows you to develop applications for your projects. You can use it to create a variety of different kinds of projects, including robots, musical instruments, and games. One of the most powerful parts of programming for the Arduino and other microcontroller boards are libraries.

A library is a collection of prewritten code that you can easily relate to with ease. These libraries contain all of the components needed to complete a specific task or series of tasks. Programmers love to use libraries because it takes a lot of the guesswork out of development, and since most libraries are free, anyone can use and modify them.

Most Arduino programmers rely on the existing libraries that come with the Arduino IDE. Some of the popular libraries include:

- **Servo** - This library will be used for controlling motors. You will want to use this library when creating robots and other machines.

- **Communication** - These libraries will allow you to connect to serial ports and digital pins.

- **Connectivity** - These libraries will allow you to connect to Bluetooth, the cloud, networks, Wi-Fi and much more.

- **Nano Family Libraries** - These libraries are used to deal with sensors and other devices.

- **Memory Libraries** - When dealing with memory, storing information, and dealing with information, you want to make sure that the data is stored and managed correctly. You don't want to have a program crash in the middle of its operations.

- **Display** - Display libraries are used to connect to LED displays, monitors, and even projectors. Even though blinking lights and signs are cool, we really want to get some information that we can understand. This is why connecting and working with displays is so helpful.

- **Audio** - Being able to play music, audio files, and more can really bring your projects to life. Think about a robot you can talk to and have it respond in a cool voice.

- **USB** - There are libraries that you can use to connect additional USB devices to. These devices allow you to add much more functionality to your projects.

- **Many more** - There are tons more that you can explore. Learning about and how to use libraries will take your development projects to the next level.

There are many other libraries available. You can search the web for more libraries and find them in your favorite online repository. For the official library repository, visit this link - https://www.arduino.cc/reference/en/libraries/

How to Use a Library in Arduino

An Arduino project consists of several files. Two types of files make up your Arduino project. The first type of file is sketches, while the second is libraries.

Why Use Libraries?

Libraries can make your Arduino projects easier to use. You can download the libraries from the internet or you can create your own. Once you have your library, you'll be able to access your library any time, from anywhere within your code.

Opening a library in your Arduino IDE gives you access to its extensive list of features.

To add libraries to your Arduino IDE, you must first click the name of the library. Then you can scroll through its features. Libraries help you add new features to your Arduino projects. There are three types of libraries:

a) **Basic**: These are the simplest libraries. They contain only a single function or macro.

b) **Library**: These contain functions that perform one or more actions. For example, you can use a library to control an LED and create a light show.

c) **Mega**: These libraries provide an environment for programming using the Arduino Mega.

Opening a Library

To open a library in your Arduino IDE, you need to click on the name of the library to make it appear in the libraries list. After you select it, you will be able to access its features. If you're using the Arduino IDE, you can easily access all of its features by opening the library list.

Using a Library

To use a library, it needs to be in your program. To do this, simply add the following code to your project at the very beginning over all other code.

include <LiquidCrystal.h>

Include - This is a command that we use when we want to add libraries and functions to our sketches. The name of the library is enclosed in < > brackets to signify that it is a library. Within the brackets, you will have the exact name of the library. If the name is misspelled, then it won't work.

Functions

When we develop a library, they are filled with different functions. In the LiquidCrystal library, you will find the following set of functions. Each function will have a specific task and hold its own code.

Functions in LiquidCrystal():

- begin()

- clear()

- home()

- setCursor()

- write()

- print()

- cursor()

- noCursor()

- blink()

- noBlink()

- display()

- noDisplay()

- scrollDisplayLeft()

- scrollDisplayRight()

- autoscroll()

- noAutoscroll()

- leftToRight()

- rightToLeft()

- createChar()

Each of these functions will now contain specific code that has variables and conditions that a developer can use. When we work with functions and libraries, our code is readable, reusable, and serves a specific function. If we were to lump all of our code into one huge file, it would not serve us in what we needed to do.

Developing Your Own Libraries

As you advance in your programming and development journey, you will develop your own libraries. When trying to determine if you need to use a library, consider whether you are ever going to use that type of code again in any project in the future. Consider writing it into a library so it can easily be included, accessed, and used. Don't try to reinvent the wheel.

Develop with Other Developers

When working with libraries, you can also work better with other developers. You can get one component working with libraries and then hand it off. The next developer can use that to take the project further, allowing new code to be written in a new library to advance the already developed features.

Chapter 10

Building Strong Programming Habits

Building programming habits that last

Development with the Arduino and other applications that you may want to try later in your journey can become very challenging if we don't learn some very basic programming and development practices. When looking at and thinking about a project that you want to create, you may think that you can simply connect a few wires, write a few lines of code and you are all set. The fact is, there needs to be a lot of thinking and planning that goes into these applications for them to work and for them to last a long time.

Microsoft Windows

When looking at programs, applications, and other tools we use daily, there is a lot of code, programming, and logic that goes into them that we never see. As an end-user, all we want to do is push a button, swipe a screen, or click on an icon and have something happen. We don't care how the milk is gathered; we just want the milkshake.

As developers for Windows, they knew that the application needed to handle everything that anyone would throw at it. Since it was the core operating system, any application that was going to work on it had to work with a basic core structure. This structure could then be duplicated with applications, and as a result, everything could work together.

Now, you see, I said "could." The reasoning for this is there are no guarantees that what a developer will write will always work with the core framework. Since it is an open platform or language allowing people to do what they want, any possible outcome would be possible. Therefore, it is important that we learn the basics of coding and have good habits from day one.

In previous chapters, we have touched on coding and programming, but now that we are going to be moving into more complex and structured applications, we felt that it would be a good idea to get your mindset right when it comes to developing a program. In the section below, we will go over in more detail how programming works, what you should expect, and how you should approach your code.

Keep It Clean

No one wants messy code. When we have spaghetti code, as it is commonly referred to, it is just a dangle of messy lines that aren't commented or structured. As a programmer, you might think you know what a section means or what you were trying to accomplish when you wrote it. However, even though you know what it is and might even be getting positive results, if your code is messy, you are not making good code.

This is why you want to write clean code. To accomplish this, you first need to ensure that you comment it. I stated this before, and I am going to stress this even more. If you don't comment your code, you are writing bad code.

When commenting your code, think of it as writing a book. You want to give as much detail and lead up to where you currently are and what your thinking is moving forward. When commenting, you can write comments in several different ways.

// This is where we want to comment on a single line of code.

/* */ When we use brackets like this, we are commenting blocks of code. The code that you write will span several lines in your application.

/* This application will discuss the way we communicate with a robotic machine that will function in the gaming industry. The result will allow a child to interact with the world around them and learn basic core skills that they can use later in life. The robot is designed for a child seven to ten years of age */

Noting Code

When writing your code, you will also want to make notations that will go to future developers.

// Richard - when working on this block of code, make sure that we connect to the RedLight // Function. In this function, I have written seven functions that we can use to develop John's // requests from the meeting.

Crediting Code

When writing your application, you will also want to give credit to others. If you use a specific function or a library, then you will want to give credit.

/* The Lightwave function developed by Robert Williams was used in this application. You can visit him at RobertWilliams.com and send him an email with any questions or concerns at RobertWilliams@CoolCodeDevelopers.com

*/

As you can see, commenting on your code can be very powerful and lets you know what is going on in your applications. As you develop more and more complicated applications, test new code and ideas, commenting will be your friend.

Write Compact Code

Next, we want to write as little code as possible when developing our applications. The reason for this is that every line of code that we write has the possibility to give us problems later in the development process. Also, when we write the same code repeatedly, we are being redundant, which can lead to errors in updating and managing our code.

When we write code, the more code that we write will also take up space on our computers, on our networks, servers, and transmitting online. When we write less code and even optimize our code, it helps with finding bugs, improving our code, and even making it modular. As you start to write code think, "How can I optimize this better?"

Indenting Your Code for Readability

As you write code, the compiler reads everything as a single line of text. However, developing our applications needs to be done so human eyes can read and understand it.

This is how the compiler reads it:

```
Void Setup(); { pinMode (13,OUTPUT); pinMode
(7,INPUT); }
```

When we write it, however, we need to have it spaced out, so it is readable and we can follow the core logic.

```
Void Setup();

{

        pinMode (13,OUTPUT);

        pinMode (7,INPUT);

}
```

As you can see in the human-readable version, we keep our code clean and aligned. When we look at the brackets { }, we can see that they are lined up, telling us what block of code belongs to what section of brackets {}. It would be a big mess if we had everything scattered around the screen. Focus on writing clean, readable code.

Variable Naming Conventions

We discussed variables previously as well. A variable is a placeholder for information that is either entered into or read from your application. For example, X can be a variable. When creating variables, you want to have the same naming convention for everyone that you use. A naming convention basically indicates how the variable looks when written.

The best way to write a variable is to either keep it all lowercase, like x or y. If it is a simple name, you will also want to keep it lowercase like buttonstate. However, if you have long variables or if you want to distinguish what your variable is, you want to use camelCase.

When we use camelCase, we break up the variable and make longer names easier to read. Also, when creating your variables, make them something that is logical. Don't have blueMonkeyGuitar as a variable name. No one will know what it means unless they know the story behind it.

Develop a Functions Library

One of the coolest things we can do when it comes to programming is develop our own library of code. These will be functions, classes, and variables that we will use over and over in any and all applications we develop. When we create a code library, we can simply include these libraries into all the applications we create and draw from code and tasks that we have done before.

When developing a code library, you want to ensure that everything is commented. You want to let those using your library know why the code was written and its purpose, and even give examples of how you can use it in your application. The more details and information that you put into your library, the more valuable it will become.

Portability

One thing that is great about programming is that when we develop in one language or in a language based on another, the code is portable and can be easily added and adapted. Since all programs use variables, functions, classes, and commenting, what we write today can be used in something else in the future with little to no effort or modifications.

Reusable and Scalable

As a developer, your main goal is to get your code to work. Your second goal is to make what you made workable reusable, and scalable. We all have ideas for applications, and we all have ideas that may be larger than we can develop ourselves. Developing our visions becomes much easier when we all program and develop with reusable and scalable code.

Testing

Testing is the key to developing a good program compared to a great one. When we develop code, you want to look at it like an adventure game or a great story in which we will have to find the treasure. The treasure in programming is having an application do what we wanted it to do and do it better than we imagined. We also want to ensure that what we write doesn't break.

When we test our code, we just don't run it once; we run it hundreds if not thousands of times. When we test our code, we are also testing it line by line. This is known as debugging.

When it comes to testing our applications, we may want to have a dedicated team of people who do this. You want to have a blind group of people who have never seen your application, have never used the application, and are not afraid to get in there and push buttons, flip switches and try to break what you wrote.

During the testing process, many people might get upset or feel that they are not good programmers if someone finds a bug or causes their code to break. This is not the case. Some of the greatest minds in the industry who stare at code day in and day out will make mistakes. When you start writing code, you will start to become blind or desensitized to what you are looking at.

Therefore, making your code portable and modular is key. When you have code that you know works, or code that does a specific task, and it doesn't, you can easily pinpoint the problem when a bug or error is discovered.

You want your testers to go through everything all at once during the testing phase. If you have a tester who finds a bug and send it off to you and then finds another, then another, it can make fixing these more difficult. Give your testers time to really go through everything and write detailed reports. You want to know what they did so you can replicate the same conditions and actions to see if you experience a bug.

Once you get your report and you start fixing things, send it back to the testers to see if they can recreate the problem. Make sure that they note that the bug is fixed, and they can move on. When working with simple applications as we have so far in this book, the need for a team of testers is not necessary. However, when you start adding more components and making your applications more complex, it is vital that you have a great team behind you to ensure that your applications work.

Becoming a Great Developer

If you want to be a great developer with the Arduino and other applications, these are some core principles you need to learn and adapt to. No one wakes up one morning and knows how to be good it takes them time, effort, and a willingness to make mistakes in order to achieve their end results.

As you continue through this book, don't become discouraged. Developing is hard, but it is also fun and rewarding.

Chapter 11

Using Serial Ports

Serial Communication: Programming With the Serial Port on Your Arduino

The serial port is a way of communicating with a computer over a serial line. The serial port is a bi-directional two-wire interface that allows us to send and receive data to and from a computer. In the past, we have been using the serial port to communicate with an external device such as a printer or a modem. However, we will use the serial port to communicate with the Arduino board.

Serial Communication Gives You a Text-User Interface (TUI)

When we look into the TUI, it means that you will be able to interact with the Arduino board using a terminal window. A terminal window will show you the board's status and allow you to change its settings. If you want to see the serial monitor, then you should open the Arduino software.

In order to see what the Arduino board is doing, you should first open the serial port. To open the serial port, click on Tools->Serial Port. This will show you the serial port window allowing you to begin communications.

Communicating with Your Arduino to Devices

You are an advanced electronics engineer, you have designed and built your own robot or maybe you are just a hobbyist who likes to build things. Whatever the case may be, you can now connect your Arduino to devices like LEDs, LCD screens, Buzzers, and other electronic components. The main thing to remember when communicating with devices is that you need to use a serial port.

The serial port is located on the computer you are using and is the means through which you can connect your Arduino to devices. The type of port you need will depend on your connecting devices to your Arduino. A parallel port will allow you to connect to devices with wires, but it is not as convenient as a serial port. In order to access the serial port, you will first need to install an Arduino-specific driver on your computer.

Sending information from Arduino to the computer

```
Var SerialPort = require("serialport").SerialPort

Var serialPort = new SerialPort("/dev/ttyACM0", {
Baudrate: 57600 });
```

The above code is a sample of the type of code you will write to communicate with your serial port. The first step is to declare a variable, var. Once you have declared it, you are required to give it a name. We will use the name SerialPort. As you can see, we camel case our variable as a good naming convention.

We then continue with the =, which is a condition. The word require is another function built into the programming language that tells us that it is required in order to work. We then give the code a parameter with the open brackets ( ), finally declaring our variable again of SerialPort.

From there, we create another variable and give it a set of conditions as well. We also declare the baud rate, which is the port and speed we will communicate with the serial port. If this number is wrong or not being used, then you will be thrown an error.

Next, you will want to use the following code block to start communications.

// it opens the connection and registers an event 'data'

serialPort.on("open", function () { console.log('Communication is on!');

// when your app receives data, this event is fired. //

This function will allow you to capture the data you are working with and do what you need with the serial port.

serialPort.on('data', function(data) { console.log('data received: ' + data); }); });

Sending Formatted Text

One function you can do is sengood-looking formatted text to your serial port. This will allow you to have bold, italics, and other features added to the text that you read. This can also be used and modified to have some fun with your text down the road. Here is some sample code that you can use to send the formatted text.

Char chrValue = 65; // Here are your values you will start with. Also, look at the code and how it is neatly structured. Try to do the same when you reproduce.

```
Int intValue = 65;

Float floatValue = 65.0;

Void setup ()

{

Serial.begin(9600);

}

Void loop ()

{

Serial.println("charValue: ");

Serial.println(chrValue);

Serial.println(chrValue, DEC);

Serial.println("intValue: ");

Serial.println(intValue);

Serial.println(intValue, DEC);

Serial.println(intValue,HEX);

Serial.println(intValue, OCT);
```

```
Serial.println(intValue, BIN);

Serial.println("floatValue: ");

Serial.println(floatValue);

Delay (1000); // delay a second between
numbers chrValue++; //to the next value
intValue++;

}
```

Receiving Data

You also have two-way communications when working with your Arduino and serial ports. This means that you can send information to the Arduino and receive it. When you receive information from the Arduino through the serial ports, you can then do tasks through code that can control other devices or perform specific functions. This opens up a lot of opportunities for development.

```
Const int ledpin = 13;

Int blinkRate = 0;

Void setup ()

{



Serial.begin (9600);



pinMode (ledpin, OUTPUT);
```

```
}

Void loop ()

{


If (Serial.available ())

    {


Char ch = Serial.read ();


If (ch >= b
```

These are the foundations that you need to start communicating with your serial ports. As you get better and experiment with the code and different functions, you will be communicating with countless devices. You will be able to take data and write to files, communicate with another Arduino and even the Raspberry PI. Take what you have learned here and start to experiment. Don't be afraid to try something new.

Chapter 12

Using Switches

In the previous chapter, we introduced you to serial ports. As we learned, serial ports allow us to send and receive data with the Arduino. With this new skill, we can now introduce additional hardware and functionality to our projects by introducing switches.

What Are Switches?

Switches are one of the simplest forms of hardware that we can use. A switch basically consists of two contacts, either connected or disconnected from the rest of the circuit. Most of the time, when we talk about switches, we mean the toggle kind, which is just a switch with two contacts, one of which is connected to the ground and the other to an external voltage source.

Switches are used to control devices such as lights, motors, or solenoids. We can use them in many different ways, but the most common way we use them is to turn a device on or off. For instance, we can use them to activate a light by switching it on or off.

Working with Switches

We can use a push button switch to control the power supply of the Arduino board. We can use a push button switch to turn on or off a lamp. We can also use a push button switch to vibrate the Arduino board.

Project Materials

In this project, we will simply be connecting a switch to your board. Here are the components that you will need to get started.

- A push button switch

- An Arduino board

- A resistor of any value

- 2 Jumper cables (breadboard jumpers)

- 1 Breadboard

- A Light Emitting Diode

Connect the long leg of the LED to pin 13 on the breadboard and the short leg to GND.

Now, connect one end of the resistor to +5 V and the other end with one of the terminals of the switch. Connect the wire from the terminal (GND) of the Arduino to the GND pin (on the breadboard) on the Arduino.

Think of terminal A and terminal B being the two terminals located on opposite sides of the airport, and they are used for connecting flights – that's how simple this is. Finally, connect the terminal with the resistor to pin 2 on the Arduino and enter the program.

The Code

```
Int d = 2;                  // to store on or off
value

Void

setup ()

{


pinMode (2, INPUT);


pinMode (13, OUTPUT);

}

Void loop ()

{


D = digitalRead (2);


If (d == 0)
```

```
    {


    digitalWrite (13, HIGH);



    }


    Else

       {


    digitalWrite (13, LOW);



    }

    }
```

Now that you have everything wired and the code is written, upload the code to the Arduino and run it. If everything works, you can press the button and get the light to turn on and off.

Taking Switches to the Next Level

Now that you have a foundation for switches, why not try to take this project to the next level? Going back to the beginning of the book, we started connecting LEDs to the board. Why not go back to that original project and try adding a switch to the mix?

When you add a switch, see if you can add multiple switches that can control different lights - have one switch turn on a red LED and another turn on a Yellow LED. Once you get these to work, try to set up a condition where when a specific color LED is on, you set a timer that will cause other LEDs on the board to flash. Improve on that by increasing and decreasing the speed, depending on which switch is hit and how long the switch was in that position.

Some Sample Code to Play With

Here is some sample code that you can use to determine how long a switch has been on.

```
Serial.println

}

If (holdTime >= 1000)

{ Serial.println

}

}
```

Create yourself some variables and what you have learned so far in the book, and use your skills and the provided code to make something happen.

Switching up a Switch with a Keypad or a Keyboard

Once you have an understanding of how to use a simple switch, you can apply the knowledge and skills with more complex devices.

One way to really take advantage of your Arduino is to connect devices such as a keypad, keyboards, and other input devices.

With these devices, we can now communicate with our Arduino in a lot more detail. With a keyboard, you can enter up to 26 letters, 10 numbers, and many symbols in unlimited combinations. Each combination gives you the power to tell your Arduino to do unlimited tasks. Now that we have this power, we can jump into creating more complex projects such as drones, cars, and much more.

For your next project, I want you to challenge yourself. Using your current skills, go ahead and use the following items and create an input device. I will supply you with some basic code to get started, but don't limit yourself.

Materials for the project

- Arduino
- 4x4 Matrix Keypad
- 8 male to male pin header

Code

The code that you will need to incorporate is as follows.

```
Char keypressed = myKeypad.getKey();

If (keypressed != NO_KEY)

{
```

```
Serial.print(keypressed);

}
```

The power of development is in your hands. The more you can focus on your end results, the more you can develop. With the examples we have given so far in this book and some sample code, you should have the foundation to do some pretty amazing things with your Arduino. In the next chapter of the book, we will be introducing the concept of movement and detecting movement. We will then take that concept and what we have also learned to start developing an actual functional device.

Chapter 13

Problem Solving and Your Arduino

The key to working with Arduino is problem-solving. When we learn how to look at a specific task and determine how we will get it to work, that is where the power of the Arduino, Raspberry Pi, and other devices shine. When working with the Arduino, our goal should be to define a specific problem, look for specific components that will allow us to solve that problem, and then assemble these parts to get us the desired result.

Understanding Problem Solving

To keep things simple, don't look at all the components and parts that you need to complete a task. Look at tasks and problems in the simplest forms. At its core, the Arduino is simply a device that allows us to send power to and from other devices. If we want to turn on a light, we simply need to run power through some wires that are controlled by a switch that tells the light if it is on or off. If you understand this, then you have the power in your hand to make these devices do anything that you want.

Describe the Arduino

The Arduino Uno is a microcontroller board that has been designed to be used in a wide variety of applications. It is a low-cost board that is ideal for learning about microcontrollers. The Arduino Uno uses the ATmega328P processor and has 16K of program memory, 8K of data memory, and a 32-bit flash memory chip. This makes the Arduino Uno suitable for a wide range of projects.

What Is a Microcontroller Board?

A microcontroller board is the small, printed circuit board that you plug into your Arduino and which is connected to the Arduino's I/O pins. The microcontroller board can be any of the boards from Adafruit, SparkFun, Mouser, or Digikey. If you want to create your own board, you can do it with any Arduino board, such as the Arduino UNO, Leonardo, or Mega, and using any of the parts available from Digi-Key, Mouser, or SparkFun.

Explain the Arduino's Limitations

The Arduino is a great platform for learning about electronics and programming. It's easy to use, it has an intuitive interface, and you can program the board itself using the Arduino IDE.

Arduinos are great tools for building electronics projects. You can use them to make cool gadgets and devices. They are cheap and easy to use. In fact, you can get started with an Arduino for only about $30. The best thing about them is that they are open-source hardware. This means you can change the code or modify the software on the Arduino board. They are great for hobbyists, kids, and adults. However, it can be hard to understand Arduino's limitations. They are programmed using C++, which is a programming language. While this language is great for writing programs for the Arduino board, it is also used to write programs for other types of microcontrollers.

When working with the board, you are going to be limited by the features and functions of that specific board. This means that you will need to add additional boards, shields, and items to the board to increase its functionality. Even though these components are usually interchangeable and easy to understand, it does add complexity to some projects as you grow your desired functionality.

Build an Arduino-Based Project

With the development of the Arduino, hobbyists and others now have the capability to make a project simpler to build by providing various pre-made shield kits to use. There are many different Arduino shield kits available on the market today. Some shields are designed for beginners, while others are intended for advanced users. When building an Arduino-based project, you can easily add shields, add components, create prototypes, and test out new ideas without having to learn how to build everything yourself. You can quickly change out one shield for another to test a different feature or function. The Arduino boards are compatible with numerous shields. When you buy an Arduino-based project kit, you can expect it to have many of the common components.

Solve the Problem

At its core, the main purpose for Arduino is to solve a problem. This problem can be anything from turning on a light to monitoring the temperature of the water in your fish tank. As a developer, simply hooking up components and running power to them won't achieve anything. Having a specific purpose and working out an idea will allow you to achieve results with the Arduino.

Circuit Paths

To solve a problem, we need to use circuit paths. These paths will allow us to determine where power is going when it is leaving, and what we need to do to control it. When designing a circuit path, think of it as a series of steps.

Step One - Action - What action are you going to perform?

In this step, whatever action you decide to do will result in an outcome. For example, if you flip a switch, what action should occur? This action will then transform into a result.

Step Two - Result - What result will occur from your action?

If you were to flip a switch, the result would be allowing power to flow through a circuit. This flowing of power through the circuit will not be your next action that then will have a result.

Step Three - Action - Power - Result?

What will be the result of the power going through the circuit? Well, it can be anything. It can be turning on a light bulb and illuminating a room or turning on a fan, television or even a digital monitor that will sense the temperature of water in a fish tank.

Step Four - Result - Action?

What will be the result and next action that you want to perform? The process of designing and programming with your Arduino will continue in this fashion. Everything that you do will be an action expecting a result that will have another action that will be a result. With this logic and understanding, we will quickly be able to create anything that we want.

The Logic and Practicality of Developing with Your Arduino

When working with your Arduino, there will be two components that you need to understand at all times. First will be the practicality of what you are going to develop and then the logic to make it work. When we can make these two components work together, programming and developing with the Arduino will be fun.

Practicality

At the beginning of the development process, we work on turning on lights, blinking in patterns, turning on and off specific lights at different times, and some other projects that aren't practical. We work on these projects simply to get a better understanding of what the Arduino can do and what it can't. These projects, however, are not really practical in real-world applications.

When thinking about and designing your projects with the Arduino, the first thing you want to consider is what the practical applications for the project are. What is the reasoning for figuring out the problem, and who will benefit from your results?

Necessity Is the Mother of Invention

The first thing you do is look at what's needed. If someone has a problem they need to solve or information they need to acquire, then this is something that you will want to design with your Arduino.

What Is Needed in the World?

This is a big question. Look at problems that you currently face and think of what you might be able to create that could benefit or assist that problem. For instance, what if you had an elderly person in your home who always forgot to take their medication? This is a problem that you could solve with the Arduino.

What you could do is create a clock-type device that would buzz or flash its lights when it came time to take their medication. You could make this project simple by having a different colored light turn on when it's time for them to take their medication - a red light for morning, blue for afternoon, green evening and yellow for night.

When they took their medication, they could hit a button that would turn off the light. You could also make this more interesting by having the light start to flash on and off if they don't take it within five minutes. You can even have all the lights flash, and a song play if it starts getting too late.

This would be a practical project that you could create. If you ever wanted to make it more powerful, have specific pills drop from a tube into a tray when the lights start to flash. This could ensure that the person took their specific pills at a specific time.

When designing projects to work with, think of practical reasons to work with the Arduino since they will give you more satisfaction in the results.

Logic

Once you decide and determine the practicality of the project, you will want to work on the logic of how to get it to work. This can be challenging but also rewarding at the same time. When working on developing the logic for your project, you want to first think of the simplest way to achieve your goal. The last thing you want to do is complicate your projects as you develop them. Work in stages and then add additional components as you go.

The First Stage

When developing the logic for your application, the first stage is to create a path of least resistance. This means you want to have an action that leads to a result. Flip a switch, and turn on a light. This is it.

When thinking of the first step in your project, don't make it complicated or long. Have a single step in the process. Once you get this step to work, then you can add another component.

Adding on with Complexity

Understand that everything that you do will add a level of complexity to your project. Adding another light, another switch, a resister, knob, LED, or whatever will exponentially make your project more complex. Now, in your mind, these additions may be simple; however, in the larger scheme of things, we are adding complexity.

Troubleshooting

Troubleshooting is where we take a step back and look at our project from a bird's eye view. We want to look at the project objectively and follow the path slowly, stopping at each point along the road to see if we are getting the result from our actions. If we are not, we need to backtrack through the process to determine where we went wrong or what stopped working.

Troubleshooting is a necessary evil when working with any type of project. If you are working with an Arduino or you are working with a sandwich, if something isn't right, we need to stop, take a step back look at everything objectively.

A common problem we encounter with our projects is that we can't always predict what will happen next. That is why troubleshooting is very important. Problems happen and we need to find a solution for them. This doesn't mean that we need to do everything ourselves. We should never be afraid to ask for advice from people who know more than us. We may be able to learn a lot from someone else who may have experienced the same issues.

Look for help

The odds are that the problem you are facing with your project isn't something new. When working with the Arduino, the project you are creating may be different; however, when we break down the project down into its core steps of action gets results, this can be a common occurrence.

When looking for help, there are many forums, Facebook Groups, and online communities committed to the Arduino and microcontroller boards. To get the best results out of these locations is to first type in a problem that you are having into the knowledge base. The knowledge base is a collection of questions and answers that have been reported to these communities. It will most likely be there if someone has had this problem or reported it in a group.

Ask Questions

Don't be afraid to ask questions. Yes, there are going to be trolls out there and people who just think they are better, but understand that we all started at the same place and advanced over time. Never be afraid to ask a question. You may find resources and like-minded people that can guide you through.

Post Solutions

When working with your Arduino, you want to post solutions projects, and even post some videos on YouTube to show people your progress. These can be amazing resources for people like you who are working with the Arduino. As a way to help encourage others to share what they know, someone needs to be a leader or trailblazer and take the first step.

Form Your Own Groups

As you learn more and more about the Arduino, form your own groups and your own communities. This will help keep you within a safe and secure bubble that you can control and will encourage others to share what they know.

Talk about Different Problems That Can Be Worked on as a Group

Sometimes there may be a project or a problem that is too complicated for your skill level or what you must work with. When looking for help and determining the logic behind a problem, post a small project and see who can join you to make it bigger or increase the scope of what is possible to create something that wouldn't have been possible otherwise.

Consider the Angle of Your Project

When determining your project's practicality and logic, consider what angle you will approach it at. Many projects that are created are often created from a practical and expense perspective. They are often people who will never actually use the product or are not the ideal customer. This is why it's vitally important to know the angle from which you will approach the project. Looking at the different angles helps open your eyes to things that could have been overlooked.

Brainstorm the Problem

Before you ever take your Arduino out of the box, the first thing you want to do is brainstorm. When we brainstorm, we are allowing our minds to open wide and are not limited by practical matters. When we brainstorm, we are open to anything and everything.

Define the Problem

A problem is anything that doesn't work properly. It can be anything, ranging from simple to complex. The problem can be a result of something else, such as the problem with the fish tank. When we define a problem, we have what is called its scope. It is the bubble that the problem lies in and what we need to do to understand what needs to be done. For example, if we need to replace a light bulb in the house, we will need to understand what is causing the bulb to burn out. This is what we would define as the scope of the problem. We would need to figure out what's causing the bulb to burn out and make a solution to address that reason.

If you are unsure about the problem, you need to define it properly. Start by determining whether the problem is internal or external. External problems are the ones that are outside the individual, such as an external force or something that affects the individual. For example, if your lawnmower breaks down, that is an external problem. Internal problems are those that are inside the individual. It could be a psychological problem, such as depression, or a physical one, such as a blood clot. Whatever it is, you need to figure out the cause of the problem and find a solution.

Identify the Root Cause of the Problem

When working with the Arduino, there are going to be two main causes for your problems. The first will be hardware connection issues. This will be that the flow of a circuit is not designed properly or not connected properly. These are usually easy to fix and can be played with easily by moving components around

The second is going to be software. The code that you wrote or use may not be well written or not connect to a specific pin or component. Software problems can be more complicated to diagnose or track down. Therefore, understanding troubleshooting and the logic and practicality of your projects are so important. Without everything working together for a specific purpose, we cannot understand if, how, or why things do what they do. Coming up With Creative Solutions

When working with Arduino, one of the most satisfying outcomes is developing out-of-the-box solutions that no one would ever have thought of before. This is another reason why Arduino is so popular. With different circuits, components, and some basic programming, we have the power to develop something that was never possible before.

Many Problems Are Overwhelming

In the world today, there are countless problems that we are trying to find a solution for. We are looking at technology with greater interest than ever before, and we are looking to make the solutions more compact and feature-rich as possible. When working with Arduino, try to come up with the simplest solution possible.

Ask Why

The answer to any problem is addressed by asking the simple question of "why".

Why does the light come on when I hit this button?

Why does it beep when I run this code?

Why does...

Asking why is a powerful tool in developing anything with the Arduino. When asking why, we start to seek out the answers and allow ourselves to be creative without solutions. If we simply take things at face value, we will never learn or advance in the development process.

Ask How

The next question that you need to ask is how. How does this work, and how can we make it better? When we ask how, we start to look at solutions in fun and innovative ways. When we ask how, we allow ourselves to think outside the box and improve on old ideas.

How do we make the light blink faster?

How do we get the red LED to turn on, then the blue LED, then the yellow?

When looking at how things are done, the next question is how can we improve on it? Just because John did a project one way doesn't mean you must do the same project the same way. This is where we really get the power of programming. Since everything is open source and everything hasn't been created yet, we can take an idea and run with it.

The Fish Tank Example

Here is the problem.

John has a fish tank that he got for his birthday. In the tank, he has a few tropical fish that he saw on a recent vacation to Florida. When he puts the fish in the tank, they start to act weird. As he reaches into the tank, he can see that the water is not warm enough to support the tropical fish.

So, John gets a heat lamp that he places over the fish tank and keeps on all day to ensure that the water gets hot. The problem with this is that John goes to school all day and doesn't come home until after four in the afternoon. If he were to keep the light on all day, the water would get too hot, and the fish could die.

Now that we have a basic scenario, we need to determine the solution to keeping the water in the tank at a specific temperature.

Identify the Solution

With the development of software and using Arduino, we have many options that we can implement. Here are a few that you might want to consider.

Timer for the Light

The first solution would be to have a timer turn the heat lamp on at a specific time of day and then turn it off after a set time has elapsed. This can easily be done with your Arduino. You could use your Arduino programmed with a timer. The timer would be set for one-hour intervals. After one hour, the lamp would turn on, run, and turn off.

This is a good solution, but it doesn't address a key point in our problem. If we simply turn on and off a light, it doesn't consider the water's temperature as a variable. Remember, a variable is a condition that needs to be met.

If we were to simply turn on and off the lamp every hour, who is to say the water needs to be warmed? We could be turning it on for longer than we need causing the water to be too erratic. This could also cause other issues for the fish. The better solution is to use the water and a thermometer or heat sensor to determine if a variable is true or false.

Use the Temperature of the Water
The better solution is to use the water temperature. How this would work is you would add a thermometer to the water or a heat sensor to the tank. This sensor would be connected to the Arduino and to the heat lamp. If the code created for the Arduino reads from the sensor that the water is at a set temperature, it will then turn the light on or off.

When we work with the water as a variable, we have a more accurate variable that will give the project a greater usability score. Not taking the water into account really defeats the purpose of the project.

When thinking of projects, make sure that you understand the need and what will be monitored. This way, you are not simply turning a light on and off but rather heating and cooling the water, which is your desired outcome.

Implement the Solution

Now that we know the scope of the project and what it is we want to achieve, we can take a step back and implement the solution. To implement the solution, we need to look at what parts and components we will need.

Parts

- Fish Tank

- Heat Lamp

- Arduino

- Bread Board

- Resisters

- Heat Sensors

- LED's

And perhaps a few other odds and ends. To create this project, we need to look at it from an overhead view.

- **Fish Tank** - This is where we will hold the fish and the water. It is the primary component of our project.

- **Heat Lamp** - We need a digital heat lamp to help us adjust the temperature. It needs to be digital since changing a physical dial would be much harder.

- **Arduino** - We need an Arduino to connect the components together and store the application code.

- **Breadboard** - We need a breadboard to have connections between all the components. We need it to connect wires to form circuits, regulators to ensure that we are not blowing up equipment, and LEDs to see if specific events are firing or if there are issues.

- **Heat Sensor** - The heat sensor is going to be key. We need a heat sensor that will determine the temperature of the water. We will use code to connect everything together and give a variable of how hot the water is. For example, if we have a variable of Water in our code and we set it to a temperature of 75 degrees. Then this water variable will need to determine if it is < greater than, > less than, or = to water. If it falls within any of these ranges, we will send a signal to turn off the heat lamp or the heat lamp.

- **LEDs** - We can have an assortment of LEDs to help us know what is currently going on with our tank. For instance, a green LED can tell us that everything is fine with the tank. We can have a red LED that tells us that the water is too hot and the lamp should be off. If the lamp isn't off, we can manually turn it off. We can have a yellow LED turn on telling us that the water is getting too cold, and the lamp should be turning on soon. If, after a few minutes, the lamp doesn't turn on, it gives us a signal to go and look.

This is how you want to go about determining what is going on with your problem. We can think of specific components that could be added to the solution and write out what their primary function will be. This also ensures that we don't overthink a project or skip over key points that would give us negative results.

Measure the Results

The final step in the process is to measure your results. When measuring the results, you can see how practical the project is and if it was worth doing. When you get your results, you can also look and see if you can make the project better. When we have an initial idea and it is all worked out, we may take a step back and have an Ah-ha moment of how it can be improved.

Maybe adding a Wi-Fi shield to the Arduino would be a good option. When hooking it up to Wi-Fi, perhaps you can get an alert sent to your phone telling you when the temperature gets to a specific level. Other options would be to add a camera to your setup and stream your fish live on YouTube 24/7.

When working with the Arduino taking the time to really think out a project and determining its purpose, logic, and more will result in cool projects that are often overlooked. Consider getting a large whiteboard or area you can write and design on. This will allow you to see a problem from an overall perspective and draw it out without constraint.

This chapter talked about setting up projects and understanding their scope. We looked at how we can create better projects by understanding their need and working out the logic. Finally, we looked at ways that we could improve on an initial idea. Take what you have learned in this chapter and sit down with a notebook.

Think of cool things that you might want to develop or go online and look for problems that people are trying to find a solution to. When working with the Arduino, we are doing it simply for fun. However, if we do come across a million-dollar idea, showing proof of concept and getting it developed into a commercial project may be a real possibility.

Chapter 14

Taking the Arduino
to the World Wide Web

So far in this book, we have really worked with local hardware and basic functionality. However, for those looking to take their Arduino projects to the next level, adding the capability to connect to the Internet will allow you to do much more with your Arduino.

What Is the Internet?

If you haven't heard, the Internet is a collection of interconnected computers that store and share resources. We do this by sending digital signals from our computers or other digital devices to a server located somewhere in the world. Then, depending on what we are looking for, the server will connect to another server or several servers before returning the requested information to us.

This connection allows us to share information such as texts, videos, audio, and applications. Depending on what we are working with, we can do amazing things. With the Arduino, we are also able to connect to the Internet if we have a Wi-Fi Shield. This shield has an ethernet connection as well as a Wi-Fi card. This means that we can hardwire with a CAT5 to the board, creating the strongest and most secure connection, or we can use the Wi-Fi connection, which allows multiple devices to connect to and from the Arduino.

How Does the Internet Work?

Before understanding why we want to have a Wi-Fi Shield installed, we want to talk about how the Internet works and why we would even want to do this with our Arduino.

HTTP - Hypertext Markup Language - This is the protocol or way anything that works on the Internet communicates. When we go to a website, we usually type http:// in front of it. This basically tells our web browser that we want to surf the Internet. When working with our Arduino, we will use this protocol in our code to communicate with the web.

HTML - At its core, the Internet is built off of HTML or Hypertext Markup Language. This language tells web browsers to display computer code into human-readable code. When designing a website or a web page, we use this code to make the sites look nice. When using the Arduino, we will be able to use this code to display things on the screen, read text and do much more.

```
<html>

<body>

<H1> Welcome to our Website! I hope you have
a GREAT Time! </h1>
```

```
<p>
```

This Website is designed to teach you how to use the Arduino. When you complete reading this site you will be a master!

```
<br>
```

```
</body>
```

```
</html>
```

As you can see, we also use special code when programming and developing websites. You can use Python, HTML, and other languages to do amazing things when programming with the Arduino. It all comes down to your creativity and your willingness to play and experiment.

Another thing that you will notice is that we have opening and closing tags with HTML. Just like with programming your Arduino, knowing and using these properly will give you the best results. This is also why developing your best practices is a good idea. Everything is transferable.

IP Address & MAC addresses

When working with your Arduino and your home Network, you will be working with both a MAC address and an IP address. These numbers will be specific for your Arduino and your home network. If these numbers don't match, then you will have issues. Look at these first if no connection is made.

MAC Address - The MAC address is your specific Wi-Fi Shield address. This number may be printed in the documentation that came with your shield and or printed on the back of your shield with a sticker. Make sure that you take note of this number; you will need it later in the code to connect.

IP Address - The IP address will be a dedicated number for your router. Each computer will have a specific number open to them that they can connect to the backdoor of their network. Usually, this number will start with 192.168.1.x. The x is where your specific number usually resides. In most cases, this number will be 255, but it could be totally random.

To locate your IP number, you want to go to your command prompt and type in IPCONFIG

Once you do this, you will see a screen pop up with a lot of numbers. You will see one that says IP Address. For mine, it says 255.255.255.255. Yours may be different. This number will be needed if you want to connect your Arduino to the network.

Connecting Your Arduino and the Ethernet Shield with Code
Once you have everything together, you will need to communicate with code. To connect your Arduino to the Internet is easy. You will simply need to use some libraries. You can get these libraries by visiting the following website.

https://www.arduino.cc/reference/en/libraries/ethernet/

Here you will have all the tools and resources you need to connect your device to the web. To connect, you will simply need to include the following two libraries.

```
#include <SPI.h>

#include <Ethernet.h>
```

These libraries will have the following classes and definitions that you can use.

Ethernet Class - This class has the following code you can use.

```
Ethernet.begin()
```

This is the code you will start all your Arduino sketches with when working with your Wi-Fi Shield. If you don't start with this code, your connection won't happen.

```
Ethernet.dnsServerIP()
```

This code is used to connect to your IP address and DNS servers. This is where you will actually start seeing information contained on the web.

```
Ethernet.MACAddress()
```

This is the code that you will use when connecting to the MAC address on your Arduino.

```
Ethernet.setDnsServerIP()

Ethernet.setGatewayIP()

Ethernet.setLocalIP()

Ethernet.setMACAddress()
```

When setting your specific numbers, these are the parameters that you will use. Make sure that when programming, you also set variables and never hardcode any numbers. If you hardcode numbers, then your programs won't work on another system, or if your numbers change.

```
IPAddress Class

IPAddress()
```

An IP address is a specific address for a website. When we want to look at websites, we are accustomed to typing in something like http://www.google.com. However, this is not the true location of Google. This text is simply masking a specific IP address, making surfing the Internet more user-friendly.

```
Server Class Server

EthernetServer()

server.begin()

server.accept()

server.available()

if(server)

server.write()

server.print()

server.println()
```

The server class is another very powerful class. This allows you to connect to a specific server and read and write information to it. This is great for the Arduino and anything else that is connected to the server. Depending on the type of information stored, we have a lot of power to work with.

These are the main classes you will start dealing with when working with the web shield. There is also a client class and two other classes that you can explore once you start learning and working with the basics.

Using the Internet

Using the internet with your Arduino will allow you to do a lot of different things. You can control actions from the Internet website, database, and more. You can even create your own web server at your home using your Arduino. Now, don't think that you will be creating the next Google or Netflix, but you will be able to connect to your Arduino from anywhere in the world and have it perform actions.

Practical Applications

So, now that you know you have this power, what can we do with it? Well, pretty much anything we can if we don't have the internet connection. However, with the connection, we can rule the world.

Home Security System

One practical application would be to create a home security system with your Arduino. With the power of your board, some tools, and the Internet you can do a lot of things.

Home Security System

This is the first thing you can do. You can watch your home while you are away. You can create a security system that takes photos of your room every ten minutes or so. This can then be uploaded to an Amazon S3 account or even a Google Drive. Then when you have time, you can easily review the photos.

Add in a Motion Sensor

Once you have your initial setup, why not add to it and include a motion sensor? This motion sensor will allow you to see if anything or anyone is moving around in your home. This is good if you have kids running around or even animals. If you are using it more for a monitoring system, you can use it to spy on the babysitter or anyone who may be cleaning or interacting in the home.

Interacting with Devices in the Home

This can be fun if you are really creative. What you can do is set up your Arduino to connect to the web and to your other devices in the home. For instance, you can turn your lights on and off with your phone. You can use it to change the channel on the television to ensure your kids are watching educational programming. You can even create a remote-control car with another Arduino, connect it to the Wi-Fi in the house, and control it, making your family believe there are ghosts in the house.

A Web Cam for Your Fish Tank

I love playing with the fish tank idea. In the previous chapter, we talked about how we could use our Arduino to monitor the temperature of the water in the tank. Why don't we take that idea and incorporate it into the web?

What we could do is hook up a camera to our Arduino and have it send signals to our makeshift web server. This video stream could then be sent to YouTube or another site where people could log in and watch a live stream of your fish.

You could also add some interactivity to it as well. Create a website or a page and include code that will connect to buttons. When pressed by people viewing the video, these buttons can send a signal to your Arduino controlling LED's, Music, camera angle, and so much more.

If you would like to see an example of using a camera as a webcam with your Arduino, go to the following video on YouTube - https://youtu.be/MicAM_A0_lU and or https://youtu.be/q-KIpFIbRMk

When using the web, we can work off our own personal network and have a closed system or connect to a live web server and our Arduino. This power opens up so many possibilities. Take advantage of ethernet connectivity and create something cool you can share with the world.

Chapter 15

Taking Arduino to the Next Level

If you have been with us up to this point, you should have a pretty good idea of what the Arduino is all about and what it is you can do with it. In this final chapter, I wanted to help you take your Arduino education to the next level. As a developer, you will want to continuously learn what is out there, what is available, and what others are doing. You will want to join communities and other like-minded groups to accomplish this.

To start, you want to go to the official Arduino Website. Here you will get all the latest up-to-date information and resources. When taking on this journey going directly to the source will typically lead you to the answer you are looking for or at least in the right direction to getting your answers.

- Official Website - https://www.arduino.cc/

- Official Website Documentation and tutorials - https://docs.arduino.cc/tutorials/

Once you have consumed all of the great official information, now is the time to jump into the community, see what others are doing, and see if you can take this firsthand information and incorporate it into your projects.

- LinkedIn - https://www.linkedin.com/company/arduino/

If you are using LinkedIn or if you are looking to get a job or join a team after you have built up your skills, then keeping this page close will help.

- Arduino on GitHub - https://github.com/arduino/

When looking for code and resources, GitHub is your go-to location for programming, code, and more. GitHub is a repository for all things code. As you explore what is available on this platform, you can open up your own free hub and start sharing your code with others. You can start building your own community of programmers and really see what is possible with your Arduino.

- Reddit - https://www.reddit.com/r/arduino/

When people have questions or want to talk about a specific topic, then Reddit is the place to go. When visiting the official Arduino Reddit page, you will have the most up-to-date questions, videos, and more to learn from. You can start by deep diving into the community, learn who is doing what, and even come up with fun and fresh ideas that you would never have thought of before.

- Hackers.io - https://www.hackster.io/arduino

If you are looking for cool projects to do with your Arduino, this is the site to visit. Here you will find a large selection of videos, projects, and more related to the Arduino. You can also go and look for other projects in different areas once you start developing your skills.

- Softonic - https://en.softonic.com/downloads/arduino

This site contains a lot of different projects and applications that you can use when developing with your Arduino. You can also explore this site for more apps and information that may interest you regarding programming and development.

- Arduino Library List - https://www.arduinolibraries.info/

As you develop, having a great library of useable code is a must. Here are many of the libraries that have been prewritten and tested to work for you. As you explore, make sure to leave comments and suggestions for new libraries. Also, come back often as new libraries are added on a regular basis.

- InfluxDB Cloud - https://www.influxdata.com/influxcloud-trial/

In the previous chapter, we talked about adding web capabilities to your Arduino. If you are looking to go even further and connect cloud-based services to your projects, then this site will set you down the right path. Understand that this site is more for advanced people looking to take their projects to the next level. You are not required to do this in your projects; it is simply a next-level option.

- Tutorial Point - https://www.tutorialspoint.com/arduino/index.htm

Looking for more information, projects, and code to use, this is yet another powerful website to explore. Here you will learn about more projects and take your ideas beyond blinking LEDs.

- Wolfram   - https://reference.wolfram.com/language/ref/device/Arduino. html

Here you will find a lot of great information on more advanced programming and development topics that you can use with your Arduino.

- Platformio   - https://docs.platformio.org/en/latest/frameworks/arduino.ht ml

Another resource for functions and libraries. As you travel through this website, see who you can connect with to build even more powerful projects.

- Components101   - https://components101.com/microcontrollers/arduino-uno

Here you can find a lot of cool components that you can use to build your next project. They have board, kits, and much more.

- Seed Studio - https://wiki.seeedstudio.com/Arduino/

If you are hungry to see what others are doing with the Arduino in practical examples, then Seed Studio will be a great place to visit. They are using Arduino to build products for the gardening niche. Check them out.

- Stack Overflow - https://stackoverflow.com/questions/tagged/arduino

If you are having problems with your Arduino, programming, or something related, you will want to go to Stack Overflow and see what is going on there. On this site, you will see what others are asking, answers to these questions and key players in this industry. If you have ever wanted a great resource for questions, visit Stack Overflow.

Amazon Kits and Components

If you want to see what can be done with the Arduino, come and check out some cool products you can get to build.

ELEGOO Mega R3 Project The Most Complete Ultimate Starter Kit w/ TUTORIAL Compatible with Arduino IDE - https://amzn.to/3PGyl52

When starting out with your Arduino, you will want to look into starter kits. With starter kits you can be assured that you have all of the correct components to get your project started and that it will work correctly. The above is a great starter kit to look into.

Official Arduino Starter Kit [K000007] (English Projects Book) - https://amzn.to/3PTNQWR

If you are starting out, you may want to consider getting this starter kit.

ELEGOO UNO Project Super Starter Kit with Tutorial and UNO R3 Compatible with Arduino IDE - https://amzn.to/3b5HiWl

Arduino Student Kit - https://amzn.to/3cHJ68r

If you want to get into the Arduino, this student kit will be a great start. It has a voltage meter so you can test how much power you are getting and sending into your Arduino. This will be very helpful down the road when you start developing more complex projects.

ELEGOO UNO R3 Project Smart Robot Car Kit V4 with UNO R3, Line Tracking Module, Ultrasonic Sensor, IR Remote Control, etc. Intelligent and Educational Toy Car Robotic Kit for Arduino Learner - https://amzn.to/3PzzStz

If you want to design a cool car that you can control, then consider getting this kit. You get everything you need and, when done, have a device you can control. We never had these cool cars when we were growing up.

Freenove Hexapod Robot Kit with Remote (Compatible with Arduino IDE), App Remote Control, Walking Crawling Twisting Servo STEM Project - https://amzn.to/3otCjBT

ELEGOO UNO R3 Project Smart Robot Car Kit V4 with UNO R3, Line Tracking Module, Ultrasonic Sensor, IR Remote Control, etc. Intelligent and Educational Toy Car Robotic Kit for Arduino Learner - https://amzn.to/3aNULlq

KEYESTUDIO Smart Car Robot,4WD Programmable DIY Starter Kit for Arduino for Uno R3, Electronics Programming Project/STEM Educational/Science Coding Robot Toys for Teens Adults,12+ - https://amzn.to/3cn7EU2

OSOYOO Robot Car Starter Kit for Arduino | STEM Remote Controlled App Educational Motorized Robotics for Building Programming Learning How to Code | IOT Mechanical DIY Coding for Kids Teens Adults - https://amzn.to/3B4gy34

Freenove Hexapod Robot Kit with Remote (Compatible with Arduino IDE), App Remote Control, Walking Crawling Twisting Servo STEM Project - https://amzn.to/3zkXEUt

OSOYOO Model 3 Robot Car DIY Starter Kit for Arduino | Remote Control App Educational Motorized Robotics for Building Programming Learning How to Code | IOT Mechanical Coding for Kids Teens Adults - https://amzn.to/3uWGidF

Robot Smart Car Board Starter Kit with Motor Tire L298N for UNO R3 Arduino PI - https://amzn.to/3RQkk6i

Premium Robot Tracked Car Chassis Starter Kits with 2pcs DC Motor, Caterpillar Moving Robotic Tank Platform with 2pcs Tracks for Arduino Raspberry Pie Microbit Python DIY Steam Remote Control RC Toy - https://amzn.to/3aSCxiQ

KEYESTUDIO Mini Tank Robot V2 Smart Car Kit for Arduino, IR Infrared and App Remote Control (iOS and Android), Light and Ultrasonic Follow, 8X16 LED Panel, Ultrasonic Obstacle Avoidance - https://amzn.to/3v1UG4q

Freenove 4WD Car Kit (Compatible with Arduino IDE), Line Tracking, Obstacle Avoidance, Ultrasonic Sensor, IR Wireless Remote Control Servo - https://amzn.to/3zkDsSI

As you can see with some of the above kits, you have a lot of different options to make something cool. When working with the Arduino, it is important that we work with kits and other components to make our lives and experiences much easier. Also, when we have different kits, we can experiment and make different items that use the same basic principles and lessons learned.

Education is key. The more time you take to learn what the Arduino can do and what projects people are doing with it, the more proficient you will become. Don't try to learn everything overnight. You will want to take your time and really enjoy playing with these devices. The more you can play and experience, the greater the projects you can complete.

Conclusion

So, we've come to the end of what is hopefully a spectacular first few steps into the great world of Arduino. Just remember, although we part ways here, this is just the beginning of your programming journey. There is so much to learn, so many exciting things to explore, and you will definitely find yourself growing as a programmer. Always remember as with anything in the world, practice makes perfect. And the more you "get your hands dirty," the greater your skills will become.

Either way, do not be discouraged by the journey you have ahead. It will be fulfilling, and you will definitely reap the rewards of all your hard work. But, every great structure needs a foundation, and so do you. Hopefully, this book has been able to give you that.

In conclusion, if you want to learn how to use the Arduino, you will need to know the basics before you start building anything. If you get stuck in a situation where you cannot progress with your project, this will help you.

Understand the scope of your project.
You need to realize that every project has many smaller components that build the whole. When we work in smaller -sized components, it is much easier to accomplish larger tasks and goals. Never try to bite off more than you can handle starting out. Look

back at the first few chapters where we sent power to the Arduino to get lights to blink. When we can accomplish these small tasks, they cement our knowledge and abilities moving forward.

Have a clear purpose

When developing your projects, have a clear purpose. What is it you are trying to accomplish? Simply plugging in wires and LEDs won't accomplish anything. You must understand the core purpose of what you want to achieve and act.

Logic

The logic of how things work is clear. Again, we have an initial action that will give us a result. That result then becomes the next action which will give us yet another result. As we develop our projects, keeping this information in the back of our hands will serve us well.

Troubleshoot

Don't expect everything to go right all the time. Their ability to troubleshoot will help separate good developers from bad developers. Don't be afraid to ask for help or look up resources online. When we do this, we not only learn what we have done wrong, we reinforce what it is we have done right.

Start small and expand

When working on a project, don't try to complete it before you even begin. It is important that we work in small chunks or sprints. We want to focus on a specific task, make it happen and then check to see if it worked. After it works, we make note of any changes we need to make to improve the initial design.

Use shields to expand capabilities

The power of shields will help you expand your initial idea into areas you may never have thought of before. When we work with shields like the Wi-Fi Shield, we are able to work with more complex functionality such as Internet connectivity. As you use shields and harness their power, the things that you can do with these boards are endless.

Build your resource library

You don't want to reinvent the wheel when working with the Arduino. You want to constantly be looking for new libraries and code samples to play with. When you get these samples, look at what they can do for you and your projects.

The key takeaway with programming is that you don't want to do things more than once. If you get something to work, create a library and store it away for future use.

Programming is difficult for beginners, so you should write the first version of your script very carefully and slowly while making sure you take everything into consideration. The last thing you want to have happen is to forget a key component and have to tear apart your project and start all over.

As you explore and grow, keep in mind that anything is possible. Find problems that need a solution and try to see how to implement an Arduino into the mix.

So go and start your adventure today. As you dive into the development process, you will learn things you never thought possible. Don't be afraid to take risks and chances. Just because something was done or written one way doesn't mean it is the one and only way to do things. Be open to experimenting and come up with something that is totally out of this world.

Good luck and, of course, have fun. Your next Arduino project is waiting for you to discover. Let the adventure begin!

Thank you for buying and reading/listening to our book. If you found this book useful/helpful please take a few minutes and leave a review on Amazon.com or Audible.com (if you bought the audio version).

References

Paul McWhorter (2019, May 31) New Arduino Tutorials

Programming Arduino Getting Started with Sketches Simon Monk ISBN: 978-0-07-178423-8

Arduino 101 A Technical Reference to Setup and Program Arduino Zero, Nano, Due, Mega and Uno Projects - Obakoma G. Martins - **ISBN-13:** 979-8698798859

Arduino Programming Tip and Tricks to Learn Arduino Programming Efficiently - Stuart Nicholas - **ISBN-13:** 979-8619761344

www.ingramcontent.com/pod-product-compliance
Lightning Source LLC
Chambersburg PA
CBHW071200050326
40689CB00011B/2198